Preferreds
Wall Street's Best-Kept Income Secret

by

Kenneth G. Winans

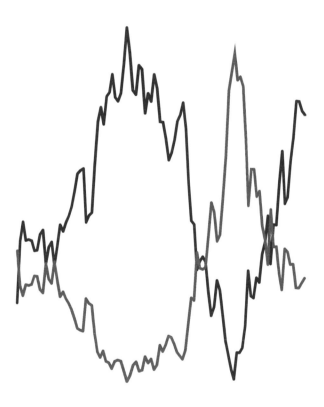

KGW Publishing

Published by KGW Publishing, Novato, CA 94949 USA
www.PreferredsTheBook.com

The amounts and percentages shown are for illustration purposes only and do not reflect actual securities or performance.

Copyright © 2007 by Kenneth G. Winans

ISBN: 978-0-9793014-8-3

Library of Congress Control Number: 2007922087

Printed in the United States of America

Cover Design: Kenneth G. Winans
Interior Design: Renée Robinson of SG&A Productions
Editor: Gary Hanauer
Copy Editor: John Maybury
Author Portrait: © 2007 Jeanette Vonier

Winans International Preferred Stock Index™ with data extensions. Price is green, yield is blue, 1890-2005. The Preferred Stock Certificate of Baltimore and Ohio Railroad was issued in 1875. It is from the author's extensive collection of documents and rare certificates of American financial history.

Of all the great, inspiring people I've crossed paths with in my life, one stands out—my father and friend, Frank G. Winans. He embodies the "American Dream" in so many respects!

Even though he is from a proud, successful family of early Dutch settlers to New Amsterdam in the 1600s, he suffered a tough childhood in the Great Depression and was separated from his family to work on a farm.

As he achieved success through his entrepreneurship and intellect, he made time to have dinner with his family almost every night. When my mother died, he kept his young family and his business

Thank you, Dad, for always supporting my efforts and dreams; this book is dedicated to you.

Love, Ken

Acknowledgments

Authors don't write books entirely by themselves.
This is my first book, so it's especially true.
A special "thank you" to the following people:

Karen Blair

Sheila Cruise

Justin Gularte

Gary Hanauer

John Maybury

Marienne McClure

Renée Robinson

Jeanette Voinier

Ty Warren

Debbie Wreyford

This book's extensive research on the Winans International
Preferred Stock Index™ was assisted by:

Justin Gularte

Vivek Jadhav

Doris Molakides

Stephanie Gliddon

The Global Financial Data Staff:

Bryan Taylor, Michelle Kangas

Table of Contents

Introduction

The Bulls Are Running!

"As between the comparatively low yields on good bonds
and the uncertainty in connection with common stocks,
investors are paying more attention to the attractive return
and security obtainable in the preferred share market."
THE MAGAZINE OF WALL STREET, SEPTEMBER 29, 1923

"Investors are showing a renewed interest in, if not a preference for, preferred stock."
THE WALL STREET JOURNAL, JUNE 16, 2005

"While exchange-traded funds already track stocks and bonds,
preferred shares might not be far behind."
THE WALL STREET JOURNAL, AUGUST 14, 2006

As the "baby boom" generation enters retirement, they are told in unison by legions of financial advisors that they must reallocate a significant portion of their portfolios into income-producing investments to generate the earnings they will need to live on during retirement. This investment shift has also been traditionally recommended to better secure the value of a retirement portfolio due to the protections offered by the issuers of these income investments.

It's easy to see the massive rush toward income investments from their strong performance since the so-called stock market "bubble" burst in 2000. Record numbers of consumers have been buying these little-understood investments, which many past investors considered to be downright boring.

Regrettably, many of these seasoned stock and real estate investors rushing into this sector of investing have failed to learn the time-proven rules of income investing and are making basic, and potentially dangerous, mistakes. Blunders such as chasing high-yield investments regardless of liquidity or maturity, believing that bonds and bond mutual funds are identical and provide similar results, grossly misusing performance statistics and agency ratings, and subscribing to a stubborn conviction that income investments are always safer and easier to understand than other investments can have grave consequences.

In fact, as an investor who has been working with income investments for 25 years, I can honestly say that the news, earnings projections, and advice from experts that we're being barraged with 24 hours a day haven't helped most investors to succeed.

To the contrary, the age old problems of successful investing still exist.

That's why I wrote this book with a single objective in mind—to make sure you're armed with useful information on how, why, and when to take advantage of preferred stocks.

Amazingly, this is the first book, since the 1930s, devoted to traditional preferred stocks—Wall Street's best-kept secret in income investing. Although it's a mystery why this time-tested investment medium has largely been overlooked, my hope is that the tips in this book will help readers navigate the world of preferred stocks and other income investments now and in the future.

Chapter 1

But There Is a Problem!

"Except under the worst depression conditions of the early '30s,
dividends were regularly paid for many years
and all Depression arrears were paid off in 1936-1937 to patient investors."
THE MAGAZINE OF WALL STREET, FEBRUARY 5, 1944

"Yes, you can get high yield,
if you're willing to take the risk of losing your entire principal
as investors go for junk-rated preferreds."
FORBES, JUNE 7, 2004

While a large number of the "talking heads" we see in the media remain focused on educating the public about investing in stocks and real estate for capital appreciation, many important issues surrounding income investing have been virtually overlooked.

History has shown that greed and ignorance cause a herdlike stampede off the Wall Street cliff during bear markets in almost any type of investment. A future market correction in income investments could cause even more damage than the bust of the dot-com bubble. The bottom line: It could literally "pay" you, as an investor, to educate yourself about the current problems facing the financial community.

Let's look at the issues at play in the market today:

INCOME INVESTING IS ALWAYS "SAFE"?

Unlike other investment mediums, income investors have fewer alternatives today than in the past; the once ample supply of corporate bonds from exchanges and brokerage house inventories have "dried up." For example, during the first week of January 1988, 1,127 exchange-listed bond issues traded; by the first week of January 2005, the number had dropped to 138 issues—an 88% decline. (CHART 1)

This dearth of individual bonds coincides with an increase in the availability of other types of income investments, such as bond mutual funds, an assortment of equity income investments and bond hybrid structures listed as preferred stocks in most newspapers. According to Standard & Poor's, the size of the preferred stock market has quadrupled in the past 15 years to nearly $200 billion.

Although equity income investments possess many advantages, they are not conventional bonds and thus don't possess the greatest advantage of a fixed income investment—a maturity date and the knowledge of an exact return, if the investment is held to maturity.

In the "old days," many income investors constructed portfolios of only bonds diversified by issuer, industry, rating and evenly spaced by maturity (i.e., laddered) with each investment intended to be held to duration. During the horrible bear market in bonds during the early 1980s, investors could maintain their discipline because they knew that, even though their bond holdings had significantly fallen in market value, they would still get their principal back, as well as their expected interest payments, if they held the bonds to maturity.

CHART 1–NYSE Listed Corporate Bonds Issues Traded
1988-2005

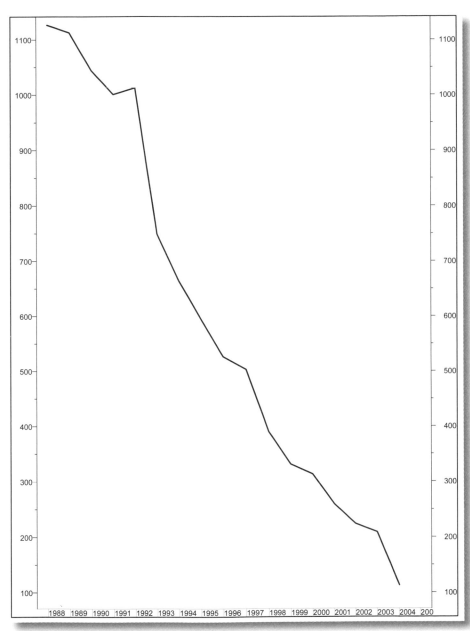

Created in MetaStock from Equis International

Unfortunately, investors have mistakenly embraced the other kinds of income investments as "apple to apple" substitutes for conventional bonds. The simple fact is that many of these investments don't mature. Open-ended mutual funds rarely hold their bond investments to maturity. When the next major market correction occurs, these hybrid securities will probably turn out to have more in common with dividend-paying stocks than with bonds held to maturity. Today's investors will get income, but not a certainty of return!

INCOME STATISTICS ARE BADLY MISUSED

When novice investors buy income investments, they are immediately exposed to new statistics, which they often don't know how to interpret. Yield to Maturity (YTM) is one of the oldest, most widely followed fixed-income statistics used. Unfortunately, many investors believe that YTM is an absolute, perfect gauge of return, so they make investment decisions based just on this one figure. However, YTM is really a theoretical total return projection that isn't based on reality. Instead, its projections tend to be too low when future interest rates increase and too high when future interest rates decline.

The problem lies in YTM's primary assumptions.
- All interest is reinvested.
- The reinvested funds are earning interest at the same rate as the original yield.

This is not realistic.
- Most investors who buy bonds are older investors who eventually use some or all the income generated (i.e., little or no income reinvestment).
- There have been very few times in the past 50 years when interest rates have been stable enough to allow interest received to be reinvested at the same rate over the entire life of even a medium-term bond.

To make the problem even worse, many financial institutions provide inconsistent information without descriptions or explanations.

On most brokerage house trade confirmations, the bond's YTM calculation is posted prominently.

EXHIBIT 1–Bond Transaction Confirmation Sheet (sample)

ABC BROKERAGE HOUSE

SAMPLE CONFIRMATION

Account Number:
Financial Consultant:

Summary For Settlement Date 01/22/2003
Total Purchases $ 14,879.27
Net Amount $ 14,879.27   Debit

You Bought 15,000 at a price of 96 ROYAL CARIBBEAN CRUISES LTD SR NOTES – BK/ENTRY-DTD 8/12/96 **YTM 8.573** 7.2500% FA-15 DUE 08/15/2006 SEE CORP/MUNI BOND NOTE BELOW SEE HIGH YIELD BOND NOTE BELOW		Gross Amount $14,400.00 **Accrued Bond Int** **474.27** Transaction Fee 5.00 Amount $14,879.27 Settlement Date 01/22/2003
Trade Date: 01/16/2003 Market: Other Markets	CUSIP#: 780153-AE-2 Symbol: RCL.GD	Solicited Order Cash Acct. Ref #: xxxx HOLD SECURITIES

We acted as principal in this transaction.

This is a sample of a brokerage house confirmation.

On most monthly brokerage house statements, only current yield percentages are used. This shows only the yield given on the monthly closing price, and is generally useless to the investor who has purchased the investment at a different price.

EXHIBIT 2–Brokerage Statement (sample)

XYZ BROKERAGE HOUSE

SAMPLE STATEMENT

July 28 – August 31, 2003

Corporate bonds

Amount	Description	Date acquired	Cost/ Adjusted cost	Share cost/ Adjusted share cost	Current share price/ Accrued interest	Current value	Unrealized Gain/(loss) Original/ Adjusted	Current % Yield/ Anticip. Income (annualized)	Ordinary Income/ Capital gain/(loss)
15,000	TENET HEALTHCARE CORP SR NOTES BK/ENTRY-DTD 1/30/1997 INT: 08.000% MATY: 01/15/2005 Exchange: NYSE Rating: BA3/BB	11/1/00	$ 14,986.25 $ 14,986.25	$ 99.375 $ 99.375	103.438 $146.66	$ 15,515.70	$ 529.45 LT $ 529.45 LT	7.734 $ 1,200.00	$ 0.00 $ 529.45
15,000	AT&T CORP NOTES B/E-DTD 6/1/1994 INT: 07.500% MATY: 06/01/2006 Rating: BAA2/BBB	11/07/00	$ 15,023.75 $ 15,023.75	$ 99.375 $ 99.375	109.875 $ 274.99	$ 16,481.25	$ 1,457.50 LT $ 1,457.50 LT	6.825 $ 1,125.00	$ 0.00 $ 1,457.50
15,000	ROYAL CARIBBEAN CRUISES LTD SR NOTES BK/ENTRY-DTD 8/12/1996 INT: 07.250% MATY: 08/15/2006 Rating BA2/BB+	01/16/03	$ 14,405.00 $ 14,405.00	$ 96.00 $ 96.00	102.00 $ 42.29	$ 15,300.00	$ 895.00 ST $ 895.00 ST	7.107 $ 1,087.50	$ 89.55 $ 805.45

This is a sample of the bond portion of a brokerage house statement.

Accrued interest is included in the cost basis of a bond on many brokerage statements and 1099 tax forms, when in fact, it is a temporary accounting adjustment that is corrected during the next payment of interest to the bondholder.

Exhibit 3–1099 Tax Form (sample)

XYZ BROKERAGE HOUSE

SAMPLE FORM 1099 for 2005

This is important tax information and is being furnished to the Internal Revenue Service. If you are required to file a return, a negligence penalty or other sanction may be imposed on you if this income is taxable and the IRS determines that it has not been reported.

1099-INT Interest Income 2005

Interest income not Included in box 3	Early withdrawal penalty	Interest on US Savings Bonds and Treas. obligations	Federal income tax withheld	Investment expenses	Foreign tax paid	Foreign country or US possession
$ 15,968.10 Box 1	Box 2	Box 3	Box 4	Box 5	Box 6	Box 7

1099-DIV Dividends and Distributions 2005

Total ordinary dividends	Qualified dividends	Total capital gain distributions	Unrecaptured Sec. 1250 gain	Section 1202 gain	Collectibles (28%) gain	
$ 8,582.46 Box 1a	**$ 2,636.46** Box 1b	**$ 2,147.33** Box 2a	**$ 320.33** Box 2b	Box 2c	Box 2d	

Nondividend distributions	Federal income tax withheld	Investment expenses	Foreign tax paid	Foreign country or US possession	Cash liquidation distributions	Non cash liquidation distributions
Box 3	Box 4	Box 5	Box 6	Box 7	Box 8	Box 9

This is important tax information and is being furnished to the Internal Revenue Service. If you are required to file a return, a negligence penalty or other sanction may be imposed on you if this income is taxable and the IRS determines that it has not been reported.

1099-B Proceeds from Broker and Barter Exchange Transactions 2005

Reference number	Date of sale or exchange (Box 1a)	CUSIP number (Box 1b)	Quantity	Description (Box 7)	Price	Gross proceeds less commissions (Box 2)	Federal income tax withheld (Box 4)
	06/15/05	527288AJ30R0	26,000	LEUCADIA NATL CORP SR SUB NTS REG-DTD 6/13/95 DUE 06/15/2005 RATE 8.250		$ 26,000.00	
	08/01/05	612448GE40B0	10,000	MONTEREY CNTY CALIF CTFS PARTN NATIVIDAD M/C IMPT PJ-C MBIA B/E DTD 10/15/94 F/C8/1/95 PREF DUE 08/01/2023 RATE 6.600		10,200.00	
	12/08/05	872384102000	165	TEPPCO PARTNERS L P UNIT L.P.	36.28	5,924.83	
	01/15/05	88033GAF70B0	25,000	TENET HEALTHCARE CORP SR NOTES BK/ENTRY-DTD 1/30/1997 DUE 01/15/2005 RATE 8.000		25,000.00	
	11/17/05	885218107000	444	THORNBURG MTG INC	25.46	11,195.74	
	12/08/05	902911106000	437	UST INC	39.54	17,137.07	
Totals						**$ 182,765.42**	

This is an exact replication of a 1099 from a brokerage house.

The current values of income investments posted on monthly brokerage statements or daily Web sites are estimated when there is no trading activity for an investment on the date shown. This can cause investors to think that there are "wild" swings in the value of an investment that never really happened!

Mutual funds provide another set of new figures, such as Average Weighted Coupon, 12-Month Yield, and 30-day SEC Yield, that make comparisons with other income investments complicated.

Sadly, the one simple figure that would be useful to most investors, annual yield (Income/Cost Basis), is not found on any information sent to a client by most brokerage houses.

AGENCY RATINGS PROVIDE A FALSE SENSE OF SECURITY

Integrated into discussions on bonds are terms, such as "investment grade" and "junk bonds," which are based on ratings issued by independent firms. Many investors misunderstand how to interpret and use the ratings on bonds, stocks, and mutual funds provided by firms such as Standard & Poor's, Moody's, and Morningstar. They often treat this information as "Manna from Heaven," without seeing the need to do any more research.

As stated in *Standard & Poor's Bond Guide*, "The issue credit rating is not a recommendation to purchase, sell or hold a financial obligation inasmuch as it does not comment as to market price or suitability for a particular investor."

It is not uncommon to find companies with good financials, having never missed a dividend or interest payment, yet they receive a non-investment grade rating. On the other end of the spectrum, ratings can be "sticky" and not decline as fast as a troubled company's or municipality's financial condition warrants. It is not uncommon to see the price of a rocky investment plummet long before its ratings do!

History has shown that bear markets don't discriminate between income investments of different ratings. In tough market conditions, most bonds and preferred stocks decline together.

KNOW THY MARKET BENCHMARK

Unfortunately, all too often the investing public blindly makes continuous head-to-head comparisons between the performance records of income investment indices and those of more liquid growth investments. Many investors then quickly change their asset allocations, based on the "race" that they somehow think is going on between the income and other investments.

As someone who constructs investment indices, I can tell you that income investment indices are as different as night and day, when compared to broader stock market benchmarks, such as the S&P 500. After all, many of the income issues used in these indices don't trade every day, so price distortions can occur. It's also important to note that most bond indices only incorporate interest when it is paid, rather than the interest that's due by the end of the year.

Although indices of income investments are useful in showing overall price trends, they are not useful as a performance gauge unless you first understand the ideas behind how the particular index was set up. Not knowing the index's assumptions can lead to false conclusions or misconceptions about performance.

Because income benchmarks are unusual, it is wise to monitor several different types from different sources to reach realistic conclusions about the historical trends of income investments.

Chapter 2

Basic Rules for Income Investing

Some Things Never Change!
*Preferred stocks listed in The Wall Street Journal
1929 and Today*

*"A great many investors find the highest grade preferred stocks, like the top grade bonds,
at prices so high and yields so low to meet reasonable objectives for income.
Nevertheless, close study will reveal that some opportunities still exist."*
THE MAGAZINE OF WALL STREET, FEBRUARY 5, 1944

*"Baby Boomers appear to be swapping growth stocks for equity income vehicles.
Thus, investment managers, investment banks and corporations
will have to rethink their current investment offerings."*
BARRON'S, APRIL 14, 2005

*"You should generally expect a bond exchange traded fund to have
higher portfolio turnover rate than the broad based equity ETF's tracking benchmarks
like the S&P 500, Dow Jones Industrial Average, and the Wilshire 5000."*
AAII JOURNAL, OCTOBER 2006

As the last section has shown, many investors handle income investments poorly. There are lots of pitfalls that investors can stumble into with devastating results. Remember, only through education and discipline can you successfully navigate the investment world over the long haul.

Before we move into a thorough analysis of preferred stocks, let's review some basic rules of investing in income investments that I have learned during my more than two decades of work in the financial "trenches."

NOTHING IS NEW

It is helpful to remember that there is very little that is truly "new" in the world of investing. Stocks, bonds, and real estate are continuously being repackaged and renamed by Wall Street, and the basic investments in the money game stay the same, even though the "it's something new" crowd seems to take center stage most of the time.

Let's examine preferred stocks and bonds. Both types of investments have been in existence for a long time. Yet some of the most technologically advanced and best educated investors in history still poorly understand the basic tenets and techniques of income investing.

Readers of this book should "start with a clean slate" and challenge their preconceptions of income investing and its relation to other investment mediums.

OWNING AND LOANING—THE CORE BASICS

When I taught graduate-level investment courses several years ago, the very first thing I told my students was: "All investing comes down to owning and loaning." "Owning" refers to investments, such as common stocks or real estate, where the main objective is to have the asset appreciate over the long term. "Loaning" is about an investor lending money to a government or company (e.g., bonds, notes, or bills), where the goal is to have consistent, secure income.

I use TABLE 1 to help set realistic performance goals for the next five years based on 15-year historical returns of various asset groups. It also helps to demonstrate how different investment types work in concert.

Compare the projected returns of two different types of $500,000 portfolios. The first is invested all in common stocks for price appreciation. The second is all in corporate bonds for income generation.

Notice that the stock portfolio has an 80% chance of producing an average annual profit of 11.7% ($58,400) over the next five years, but the bond portfolio held to maturity has 95% odds of making an average annual profit of 9.1% ($45,363) in the next five years. To the novice investor, the choice would be simple: "Put me in 100% common stocks."

However, other factors need to be considered to meet all of an investor's expectations.

TABLE 1–5-Year Porfolio Performance and Asset Allocation Projections

5 Year Portfolio Performance Goal & Asset Allocation Projections								December, 2005
15 Year Total Annual Returns (%):		Cumulative:	Annual:	Calculation:	Success Probabilites:	Goal:		
S&P 500 Index		18.6%	10.6%	14.6%	80.0%	11.7%		
Dow Jones Corporate 20		7.6%	11.5%	9.6%	95.0%	9.1%		
	Stock Asset Allocation	Bond Amount	Bond Asset Allocation	Portfolio Goal	Portfolio Success Probabilities	Capital Gains $	Income $	Average Annual Return $
Stock Amount								
$500,000	100%	$0	0%	11.7%	80%	$48,400	$10,000	$58,400
$0.00	0%	$500,000	100%	9.1%	95%	$0	$45,363	$45,363

A Need for Greater Certainty of Return

Although it is common for the investment community to set an investor's asset allocation based mainly on how old they are, I have found that an investor's personality and temperament have more to do with the investment mix of a portfolio than their physical age.

In essence, many people, regardless of age, can't handle high investment uncertainty and will panic and abandon a time-tested investment strategy at the first signs of trouble.

With a 20% possibility of not meeting expected goals, along with the fact that the S&P 500 Index performed in negative territory 25% of the time since 1973, income investments can be attractive choices for low-risk investors.

What Type of Portfolio Profit Is Needed?

For investors who need to regularly withdraw funds from a portfolio, the type of investment profit is an important consideration.

In a stock portfolio, most of the expected profits are in the form of capital gains ($58,400 annually in the previous example) that would require the selling of an investment or borrowing on margin for an investor to access the needed funds. Furthermore, because stocks historically have negative years a quarter of the time, there would probably be instances when a stock investor would need to withdraw funds when his or her portfolio is at a low point, thereby selling investments at less than opportune times.

On the other hand, the bond portfolio's profits are in the form of income that arrives at regular, predictable intervals and can be accessed without changing the investor's holdings.

Taxes

Historically, the government has treated profits generated by investments differently because interest income is typically taxed at a higher level than gains realized by selling an investment. There are many time-tested techniques that can minimize taxes in an income portfolio, such as using municipal bonds, tax loss selling, bond swaps, and amortizing premiums. Investment strategy and tax planning need to go hand in hand for the best investment results.

There is no such thing as a "single best" investment! Although there's no doubt that stocks can generate more wealth than bonds over time, their profitability can't be guaranteed. Many income investments can provide a projected and issuer guaranteed return due to the regular payment of income and set dates for the repayment of principal.

MANY BOND MARKETS

I can't count the number of times I've heard this statement on a financial news channel: "Stocks and bonds were up today!" Although the commentary might seem accurate, often the type of bonds aren't disclosed. Are they U.S. Treasury, municipal, or corporate bonds?

Although it is true that all bonds are generally affected by the level and direction of interest rates, each type is greatly influenced by different, independent factors. For instance, treasury bonds are affected more by the buying and selling of U.S. government bonds by central banks in other countries. Tax-exempt municipal bonds are influenced more than other bonds by changes in federal and state tax laws. Corporate earnings projections can affect common stocks, preferred stocks, and corporate bonds alike.

The following 105-year yield spread charts show the differences between yields of preferred stocks versus corporate bonds and preferred stocks versus 90 day T-bills (Charts 2, 3). The charts show very wide swings in the yields of the three

CHART 2–Preferred Stock Yield versus Moody's Corporate Bond Yield (Spread)
1900-2005

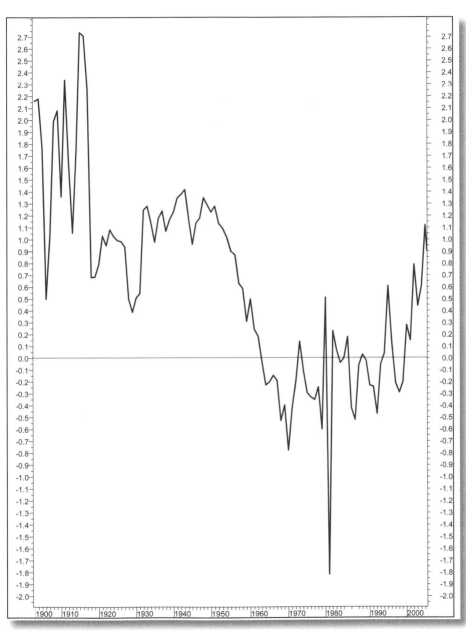

Created in MetaStock from Equis International

CHART 3–Preferred Stock Yield versus 90 Day T-bill Yield (Spead)
1900-2005

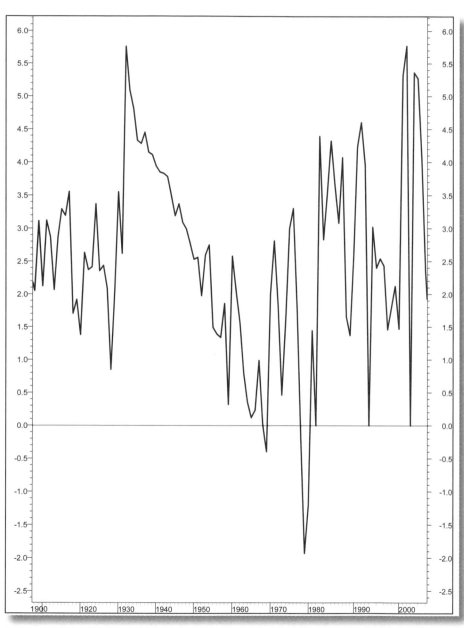

types of investments, relative to one another. Clearly there are times in which an investment in one medium would provide a better relative yield than another.

The truth is, that instead of there being a single bond market, there are markets for various types of income investments. Not all investments are the same!

INCOME INVESTMENT COSTS

There are primarily two types of costs associated with income investing: transaction fees and management fees.

Transaction Fees

Everything bought or sold in the investment world has costs associated with the services provided by the brokerage houses. There are common instances where investors are not aware of or are confused about what income investments actually cost to trade. It is not unusual for an investor to be told that investments bought from the brokerage house's own inventory "has no commission costs," and thus the client thinks the trade was done for "free." The truth is that the investments' prices were probably "marked up," and similiar investments may have been bought cheaper at another brokerage house. Keep in mind that income investments can be easier to buy than to sell, so make sure the brokerage house holding your investments can buy and sell your holdings for a reasonable price.

Like any other large purchase, it is wise to shop around for the best deal.

Management Fees

Generally speaking, most professional money managers have different levels of fees based on the type of investments. It is standard practice for managed income portfolios to be charged at a lower rate than portfolios of common stocks. Fees charged for managing municipal bonds are usually not tax deductible.

DIVERSIFICATION

Over the past 60 years, there has been very little debate between investment professionals and academia on the need for investment diversification within a portfolio. Diversification, among other things, reduces the negative impact of a single investment on the entire asset base. However, disagreements on how to diversify are common. Sadly, diversification is often misused for marketing purposes by unethical members of the investment community to sell unneeded investments.

Diversification within a portfolio of income investments is much more complicated than for other types of investments. In addition to diversifying by issuer, capitalization, and industry, the income investor also needs to consider maturity (i.e., duration), investment type (government debt, corporate bond, preferred stock, etc.) and agency ratings. In my experience, improper diversification or no diversification at all in income investing is common and can lead to unknown risk and lost opportunities. This is especially true when it comes to the sole use of agency ratings or issuer guarantees as a means to building an income portfolio.

INVESTING'S TWO BIGGEST DANGERS

History has shown that any investor can "blow up" a portfolio with any type of investment if he or she leverages it high enough or use too many illiquid investments. Such a situation will be exacerbated when a normal-to-severe bear market occurs.

Leverage

Many investors have successfully used margin loans and mortgages to enhance returns and withdraw equity from fully invested portfolios. And they can be the seeds of destruction for those who don't pay attention to the saying that "too much of a good thing can be bad." Repayment guarantees won't protect you if you suffer a loss in market value from highly leveraged income investments and your broker or banker forces the sale of your leveraged holdings at the worst of times.

Illiquidity

Liquidity is the ability to buy and sell an investment quickly at a reasonable price. In the universe of income investments, liquidity spans from excellent to nonexistent with illiquid investments generally offering much higher yields than liquid investments. As a general rule, investors should limit their exposure to non-liquid investments while planning to keep all of their income investments for the long term. It is also important to avoid the temptation to trade for short-term gains or cut short-term losses based on prices posted on a statement or a Web site. There is a good chance the numbers are not accurate due to low trading activity (i.e., illiquidity). Finally, do not normally use stop loss orders with income investments. Due to frequent sudden gaps in prices, it's a sure way to lose money (Chart 4).

CHART 4—Bear Stearns pf - X "Price Gaps"
2005

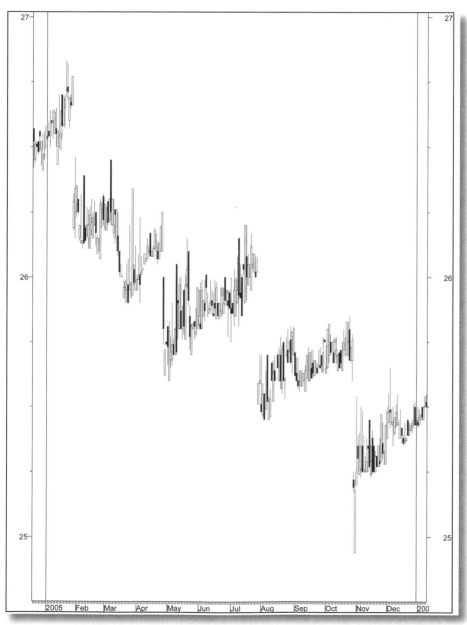

If the greatest advantage of owning income investments is providing a projected and guaranteed return through its payment of income, then reducing the risks discussed above and proper diversification should be followed at all times.

If you feel the need to gamble, then go to Las Vegas—don't use your investment portfolio!

INFLATION, TAXES, AND THE U.S. DOLLAR

Although investors often happily focus on the price movements of profitable investments, most give only passing thoughts to the influence of inflation, taxes, and the value of the U.S. dollar on long-term performance. This is particularly true of income investments!

Inflation

Because the prices of income investments are not expected to appreciate in the long term, an income investor will have to do one of two things to combat inflation.

- Own other investments that perform well above the expected inflation rate.
- Reinvest some of the annual income into more income investments.

A dollar today and a dollar tomorrow are not the same value. In fact, every 10 years the value of money historically loses 10% to 15% of its real value. If steps are not taken to minimize the effects of long-term inflation, an income investor will receive significantly less real income in the future.

Taxes and Account Placement

The government has typically treated profits generated by investments differently, with investment income typically taxed at a higher level than gains realized by selling an investment. Because an investor can't control when he or she is paid interest or dividends, tax-deferred accounts (such as retirement accounts or annuities) are ideal for holding taxable income investments, because the investor isn't taxed until the money is withdrawn from the accounts.

One of the best examples of blindly using income investments without understanding the basic differences between the various types may occur when an investor places municipal bonds or municipal bond mutual funds into a tax-deferred account. Because the investment account type matters, tax-free yields may lose their benefits, depending on the type of account selected.

Remember, investment placement can have important implications on after-tax returns!

U.S. Dollar

More and more Americans have been investing outside of the U.S., and many investors have been adding foreign income investments to their portfolios. Sometimes, investors chase after foreign bonds because they have higher nominal yields than similar U.S. bonds. But what some investors forget is that the interest payments made on most of those bonds are in the currency of the issuer's country. A dramatic change in the value of that currency can cause a loss of true income after the interest is converted back into U.S. dollars.

INTEREST RATES AND INVESTMENT RETURNS

Interest Rates

As can be seen on the chart of interest rates on 90 day T-bills over the past 50 years, it can easily be said that they are not stable (CHART 5). In fact, in the last seven years we have seen short-term (Fed funds) rates swing 12% due to the Federal Reserve's attempt to influence investment valuations in a relatively inflation-benign environment.

It is important to note that the market value of income investments is more directly affected by changes in overall interest rates than all other investment mediums.

The relationship is very simple. When the Federal Reserve raises interest rates, the current price of an income investment usually goes down. And when the Fed lowers interest rates, the current price of an income investment typically rises. Unfortunately, this situation sometimes clouds the true long-term performance of income investments.

By the way, in an environment where there is an inverted yield curve between short- and long-term interest rates (i.e., short-term rates are higher than long-term interest rates), an income investor should be more cautious and stick to new investments with shorter maturities.

CHART 5–90 Day T-Bill Yields
1950-2005

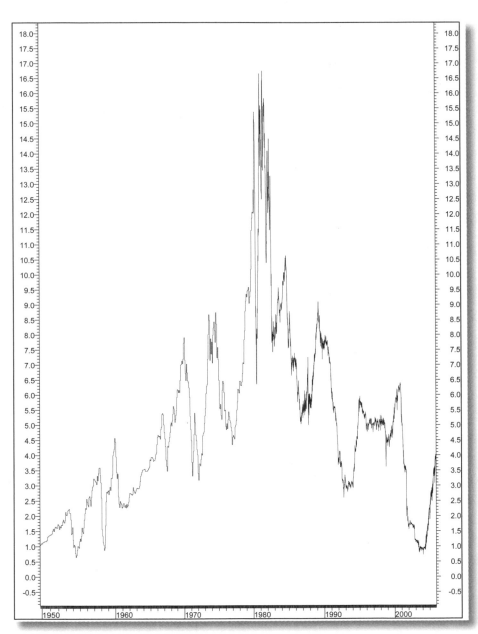

Created in MetaStock from Equis International

Investment Returns

If the original purpose of "loaning" is to provide an investor with a projected return due to its regular payment of income and set date of the repayment of principal (i.e., near certainty of return), then one must ask why the current price of an income investment is of any importance unless an investor wants to acquire more of or wishes to sell the investment.

Furthermore, is it of any value to review an income portfolio or an index of income investments quarterly because much of the portfolio's projected income isn't paid until the last quarter of the year?

Ultimately, it is a question of which is more important—annual returns or the cumulative returns since the investment was first made.

To measure the performance of income investments, I use the following reports. EXHIBIT 4 is for bonds and EXHIBIT 5 is for income stocks (such as preferred stocks, real estate investment trusts, energy partnerships, etc.).

This format is very useful and provides information usually not available on brokerage statements. When looking at the report, there are several ways to review the overall performance of this income portfolio:

Market Value and Par (Maturity) Value

In comparing the market value with the par value at the bottom of the table, you will notice that the bond holdings are currently worth more at maturity than if they were to be liquidated today. Remember that par value is a legal obligation that the issuer owes the holder of these bonds at maturity, so market value is of less use than for a common stock owner.

Annual Yield and Year to Date Price Change

The "Annual Yield" (projected income for the year/cost basis) shows the percentage earned from interest paid in a year. This is different from the YTM calculation, which assumes the reinvestment of all income.

The "Year to Date Price Change" measures the change in the price of the investment for the current year. For example, both reports show the market value of the investments has dropped since the beginning of the year. However, if the prices do not decline any further, the total return (Annual Yield +/- YTD price change) of the portfolio will be positive after all income is collected by the end of the year. A common mistake is to compare a bond's annual price change to a market benchmark without including the estimated income.

Cumulative Change in Price versus Cumulative Income Received

Since the bond investments in this portfolio have been purchased, they have declined $7,747 in value. And they have also produced $74,608 in interest payments over the same time frame. The investments have indeed been profitable to own!

EXHIBIT 4—Performance Report (Corporate Bonds)

See Disclaimer

Description	Market Value	Par Value	Annual Yield %	Year to Date Change %	Cumulative Change $	Cumulative Income
Corporate Bonds						
CORPORATE BOND 7.5% 02/15/11	$25,470	$25,000	7.5%	-0.2%	$465	$1,808
CORPORATE BOND 7.2% 07/15/08	$15,559	$25,000	7.1%	-1.9%	$60	$7,042
CORPORATE BOND 7.75% 03/01/07	$6,053	$6,000	7.5%	-1.9%	($113)	$2,744
CORPORATE BOND 9.05% 11/15/11	$26,013	$24,000	8.1%	-2.1%	($843)	$4,630
CORPORATE BOND 7.875% 07/15/13	$11,220	$12,000	7.9%	-9.2%	($766)	$7,826
CORPORATE BOND 7.625% 5/15/0	$25,563	$25,000	7.3%	-2.0%	($723)	$7,458
CORPORATE BOND 7.75% 02/1/10	$15,000	$15,000	7.7%	-4.3%	($103)	$4,255
CORPORATE BOND 9.375% 06/01/11	$15,675	$15,000	9.1%	-0.2%	$259	$4,369
CORPORATE BOND 8.75% 07/15/07	$21,394	$21,000	8.2%	-2.0%	($927)	$15,593
CORPORATE BOND 8.25% 12/15/11	$24,750	$25,000	8.3%	2.1%	($5)	$1,712
CORPORATE BOND 10.75% 10/15/06	$8,150	$10,000	10.5%	-19.3%	($2,136)	$1,496
CORPORATE BOND 6.5% 08/15/10	$23,500	$25,000	6.7%	-1.8%	($755)	$1,345
CORPORATE BOND 7.75% 03/15/13	$45,360	$48,000	7.4%	-3.4%	($4,975)	$5,668
CORPORATE BOND 7% 05/01/12	$15,525	$15,000	6.9%	-1.4%	$380	$3,153
CORPORATE BOND 6.85% 06/01/08	$9,135	$9,000	7.1%	-1.5%	$494	$2,809
CORPORATE BOND 6.0% 01/04/14	$28,050	$30,000	6.9%	-6.5%	$1,940	$5,701
Corporate Bonds Subtotal	**$326,416**	**$330,000**	**7.8%**	**-2.9%**	**($7,747)**	**$74,608**

Notice that the information is nearly identical for equity income investments, except I didn't include par value because they don't have meaningful maturity dates. Some equity income investments have dividend yields that can fluctuate over time, so the "Dividend Yield %" is an estimate based on the average of the past two years of dividend payments. As was seen with the bonds, the values of the investments have dropped since being purchased ($13,526) and the dividends collected over the same period were a higher amount, $32,596.

EXHIBIT 5—Performance Report (Income Stocks)

See Disclaimer

Description	Shares	Market Value	Average Div. Yield %	Year to Date Change %	Cumulative Change $	Cumulative Income $
Equity Income						
COMMON STOCK	865	$26,132	7.9%	2.9%	$1,094	$1,603
PREFERRED STOCK 8.7%	887	$24,295	7.1%	0.3%	($2,907)	$3,647
PREFERRED STOCK 8.00%	949	$24,627	7.5%	-0.9%	($579)	$3,588
PREFERRED STOCK 8.6%	956	$24,311	8.2%	-3.6%	$897	$1,064
COMMON STOCK	221	$9,724	8.0%	14.3%	$2,143	$1,700
PREFERRED STOCK 8.765%	838	$21,646	7.9%	0.4%	($1,754)	$3,485
PREFERRED STOCK 8.3%	848	$22,345	7.3%	-30.5%	($2,994)	$2,934
PREFERRED STOCK 8.125%	919	$23,591	7.4%	-1.9%	($1,710)	$4,953
PREFERRED STOCK 7.25%	284	$7,214	6.7%	-0.5%	($414)	$1,738
COMMON STOCK	276	$9,748	5.2%	-19.0%	($2,896)	$535
PREFERRED STOCK 8%	282	$26,085	10.1%	4.3%	$1,066	$56
PREFERRED STOCK 9%	950	$24,064	8.4%	0.3%	($1,425)	$5,675
COMMON STOCK	1,335	$21,654	8.4%	0.2%	($2,255)	$1,618
Equity Income Subtotal		**$265,433**	**7.7%**	**-3.8%**	**($13,526)**	**$32,596**

In summary, there are many ways to evaluate the performance of an income portfolio. Because all investments are distinctly different, there is no single, uniform way to analyze every investment.

Ultimately, successful investment performance should be based on meeting a realistic expectation, not in comparing what your friends and neighbors are doing with their money. **Investing is a journey, not a horse race!**

INCOME MUTUAL FUNDS

For the last 50 years, mutual funds have been a popular way to invest in stocks and bonds. For income investing, municipal bond funds are the most popular, with more than 615 open-end and 278 closed-end funds to choose from, as of 2007.

And, just because something's popular doesn't mean it's the best way to invest. If a projected return, through a regular payment of income and set date of the repayment of principal, is the greatest advantage of owning fixed income investments, then many mutual funds miss the mark.

TABLE 2–Mutual Funds Annual Performance and Market Yields Comparision (1991-2005)

Mutual Fund Annual Performance and Market Yields Comparision (as of 12/30/2005)					
	Total Returns			Trailing 12 Months	
Investment Catagories:	15 yr	10 yr	5 yr	Asset Turnover	Expense Ratio
US Corporate Bond Funds	7.0%	5.5%	5.3%	135%	0.83%
Moody's Corporate Bond Yields	8.7%	7.5%	7.5%	0%	0.00%
Difference	**-1.8%**	**-2.0%**	**-2.2%**		

Source : Winans International, Morningstar

Here are some things to consider before investing in bond mutual funds:

Asset Turnover

Bond funds have been known for having the highest amount of annual turnover (i.e., trading) of any type of mutual fund. TABLE 2 shows that corporate bond funds with more than $50 million in assets had an average portfolio turnover of 135%. A bond portfolio of non-callable issues evenly laddered over 10 years would imply that only 10% of the portfolio would come due every year, so the high turnover ratio suggests that the funds are actively trading bonds (i.e., not holding investments to maturity), which means they could be giving up one of income investing's best advantages.

Bond Mutual Funds Versus Buying and Holding Bonds

The trading activity described above can be justified only if it produces better returns than directly buying and holding income investments to maturity. TABLE 2, a comparison of the average 15-, 10- and 5-year returns of corporate bond funds with more than $50 million in assets was made and compared to Moody's corporate bond yield average during the same period of time. Because the bond yields were noticeably higher than the mutual fund group's average return in each time category, an investor should consider that buying and holding a portfolio of bonds directly could produce better overall returns than those found in investing in most corporate bond funds.

Finally, it is not uncommon for mutual fund investors who own an assortment of funds to think they are properly diversified. Remember that many funds own bonds from the same issuers.

Open-End Versus Closed-End Funds

Although they are all considered mutual funds, they are structured and managed differently. In general, closed-end funds (which includes their close cousin, exchange traded funds) typically have lower turnover ratios and fund related costs than open-end funds.

Management Fees

The average corporate bond fund fee in 2005 was .83%. This needs to be incorporated into any comparison with the low cost of buying and holding income investments directly. Remember that these fund management fees do not include sales loads, 12b-1 fees, and transaction expenses resulting from asset turnover.

Monthly Income

Many funds offer investors the ability to receive a monthly income instead of having to wait for income investments to pay dividends quarterly or interest payments semi-annually.

Account and Transaction Size

With discount brokerage houses offering more income investments, an investor with as little as $75,000 can invest directly in a well-balanced income portfolio of approximately 15 bonds or equity income securities. Also, it is not uncommon for investors to start with bond funds and convert their portfolio to direct investments after their portfolio reaches a larger size.

Summary

Many investors have mistakenly embraced income investment products, including mutual funds, as equal substitutes for buying and holding conventional bonds. In reality, a large number of these investments don't mature and or provide a projected rate of return. In the next major market correction in income investments, a painful truth will emerge—these investments have more in common with dividend-paying stocks than bonds held to maturity. Simply put, investors are getting income and not a certainty of return.

36 Preferreds

Chapter 3

Preferred Stocks,
A Wall Street Orphan

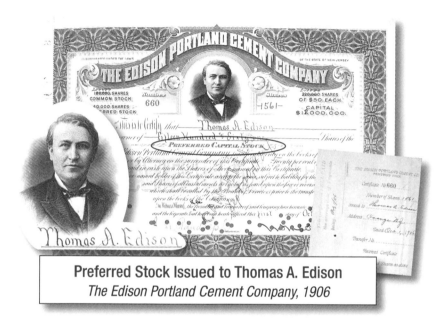

Preferred Stock Issued to Thomas A. Edison
The Edison Portland Cement Company, 1906

*"It is sometimes said that preferred stocks provides more liberal yield than bonds
and a greater certainty of income than common stocks.
From another viewpoint, the preferred stock possesses some of the disadvantages
of both bonds and common stocks without all the advantages of either.
At least the advantage of each of the two classes
is not possessed by preferred stock unrestrictedly."*
INVESTMENT FUNDAMENTALS, ROGER BABSON, 1935

"Even stockbrokers have difficulty getting the facts on preferreds."
FORBES, MARCH 3, 2003

*"While preferred shares are listed on major stock exchanges,
they aren't widely followed or understood—so there's a chance to unlock hidden value."*
THE WALL STREET JOURNAL, AUGUST 6, 2006

Rarely is there an opportunity to conduct exploratory research on one of Wall Street's cornerstone investments. It is somewhat of a mystery why preferred stocks, one of the oldest and most reliable exchange listed investments in existence, would "fall between the cracks" in a global investment industry overly fixated on constructing market benchmarks and offering the investing public as many investment products as possible.

Even more interesting is the extreme range of opinions expressed by the media on the rare occasions that preferred stocks are even mentioned. For instance, *Forbes Magazine* has had articles titled "Dull is Good: Preferred Stock" and "How to Buy a Preferred," and one of its senior columnists wrote in the book *The Wall Street Waltz*, "Common stocks offer appreciation, while preferreds offer nothing at all."

In this section, the Winans International Preferred Stock Index™ (WIPSI™) will be reviewed. It is important to note that the WIPSI is the first investment index created that is devoted to tracking the price and yield of traditional preferred stocks.

Investment research should be timely and insightful. This chapter meets these requirements because:

- At press time, preferred stocks were trading near 25-year price highs. The timing is perfect for investors to regauge the risk of buying and holding these investments (CHART 6).
- Equity income investments (preferreds, REITs, listed partnerships, etc.) and the increased number of hybrid investments created by the investment industry have grown in popularity. In fact, both *The Wall Street Journal* and *Barron's* have recently added "Preferred Stock" sections to their publications and Web sites.
- Since December 30, 1980, the WIPSI has had a cumulative total return of 407% and an average annual total return of 14% versus The Dow Jones Corporate Bond 20 Index's 262% cumulative and 12% annual return (TABLE 3). Simply put, there is evidence that preferred stocks can be a better investment than corporate bonds!
- Very little technical and fundamental investment research has ever been conducted on these investments.

CHART 6–WIPSI
1980-Present

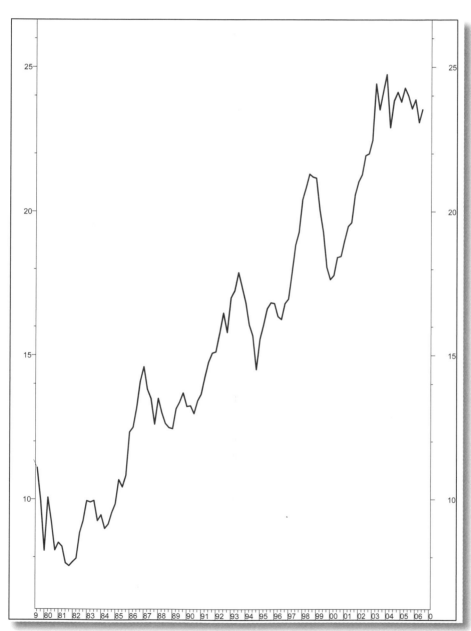

TABLE 3—WIPSI™ and Dow Jones Corporate Bond 20 Index Annual Returns
1981-2005

WIPSI

Year-end	Index Value	Yr to Yr % Change	Beginning of Year Yield	Total Return
1980	8.58			
1981	7.99	-6.9%	13.61%	6.73%
1982	9.62	20.4%	14.79%	35.19%
1983	9.63	0.1%	12.36%	12.46%
1984	9.88	2.6%	12.46%	15.06%
1985	11.19	13.3%	12.18%	25.44%
1986	14.57	30.2%	10.65%	40.86%
1987	12.93	-11.3%	8.69%	-2.57%
1988	12.81	-0.9%	9.77%	8.84%
1989	14.04	9.6%	9.76%	19.36%
1990	13.76	-2.0%	8.96%	6.97%
1991	15.46	12.4%	9.12%	21.47%
1992	16.2	4.8%	8.09%	12.88%
1993	17.75	9.6%	7.69%	17.26%
1994	14.84	-16.4%	6.97%	-9.42%
1995	17.19	15.8%	8.58%	24.42%
1996	17.17	-0.1%	7.49%	7.37%
1997	19.64	14.4%	7.50%	21.89%
1998	21.49	9.4%	6.69%	16.11%
1999	18.34	-14.7%	6.23%	-8.43%
2000	18.71	2.0%	7.43%	9.45%
2001	20.82	11.3%	7.34%	18.62%
2002	22.19	6.6%	6.97%	13.55%
2003	24.34	9.7%	6.98%	16.67%
2004	24.41	0.3%	6.29%	6.58%
2005	23.78	-2.6%	6.28%	3.70%
Average		4.7%	8.7%	**14%**
Cumulative Change		184.5%	222.9%	**407%**

Dow Jones Corporate Bond 20 Index

Year-end	Index Value	Yr to Yr % Change	Beginning of Year Yield	Total Return
1980	88.59			
1981	79.41	-10.4%	12.9%	2.5%
1982	98.29	23.8%	14.8%	38.6%
1983	97.03	-1.3%	12.1%	10.8%
1984	100.79	3.9%	12.4%	16.3%
1985	116.47	15.6%	12.3%	27.9%
1986	129.98	11.6%	10.5%	22.1%
1987	120.82	-7.0%	9.3%	2.3%
1988	123.24	2.0%	10.3%	12.3%
1989	129.29	4.9%	10.0%	14.9%
1990	127.39	-1.5%	9.3%	7.8%
1991	137.35	7.8%	9.5%	17.3%
1992	143.72	4.6%	8.5%	13.1%
1993	145.86	1.5%	7.3%	8.8%
1994	130.16	-10.8%	6.2%	-4.6%
1995	146.53	12.6%	8.2%	20.8%
1996	144.37	-1.5%	6.9%	5.4%
1997	146.14	1.2%	7.2%	8.4%
1998	147.96	1.2%	6.9%	8.1%
1999	135.82	-8.2%	6.5%	-1.7%
2000	135.44	-0.3%	7.8%	7.5%
2001	143.69	6.1%	8.1%	14.2%
2002	159.23	10.8%	7.3%	18.1%
2003	174.68	9.7%	5.5%	15.2%
2004	185.23	6.0%	4.7%	10.7%
2005	188.48	1.8%	4.9%	6.7%
Average		3.4%	8.8%	**12%**
Cumulative Change		42.5%	219.4%	**262%**

WHAT IS A "PREFERRED" ANYWAY?

Preferred stocks are unique in many ways.

Fixed-Rate Dividends Paid Indefinitely

Although they are considered to be equity, these securities are usually compared with fixed-income investments. This is because, like bonds, most preferred stocks promise to pay a specified stream of income. Unless there is a call provision, a sinking fund or a floating rate, preferred stocks will pay an established dividend in perpetuity. Most preferred dividends are paid quarterly and are subject to the same rules about ex-dividend dates as common stocks.

Unpaid Dividends Usually Cumulate

Unlike bonds, the failure to pay the promised dividend does not result in corporate bankruptcy. Instead, the owed dividends of traditional preferreds accumulate and the common stockholders may not receive any dividends until the traditional preferred stockholders have been paid in full. Preferred stocks rarely give their holders full voting rights, but if a dividend is missed, the shareholders will be provided with some voting power.

Share Price

Most preferred stocks start trading or are called at $25, $50, and $100 per share (i.e., par value). Preferred prices rarely split.

Convertible To Common Stock

Many preferreds will allow investors to exchange their preferred stock for common stock (at a preset price and share amount). And, this opportunity usually comes at the cost of a substantially lower dividend yield than offered on conventional preferred stock.

Specific Issuers

Utilities, financial companies, real estate investment trusts, railroads, manufacturers, and companies with a large number of subsidiaries are the main issuers of these securities.

Dividend Tax Treatment

Certain types of preferred stocks can qualify for a significantly lower tax rate (15% versus 35%) for individual investors called Qualified Dividend Income (QDI). Corporations that buy preferreds can get special tax deductions called intercorporate Dividends Received Deduction (DRD).

Many years ago, one of my clients, who grew up on a farm, told me that he viewed all investments like owning cows. Some were owned for their meat (appreciation) and others were used to produce milk (income). While they are both important to a farm or ranch, they each serve a very different purpose. This turned out to be a great analogy of common and preferred stocks together in a portfolio.

WHERE TO FIND THEM?

Like most common stocks, preferreds are listed on major exchanges and can be purchased at most brokerage houses. *The Wall Street Journal* and *Barron's* publish lists of actively traded preferred stocks in their investment tables. And various Web sites, such as www.PreferredsOnline.com, post the trading activity of preferred stocks.

PREFERRED STOCK LONG-TERM PERFORMANCE

To review the long-term performance of preferred stocks, several studies had to be combined: Mitchell Preferred Stock Average (1890-1929), S&P's preferred stock studies (1929-1980), and Winans International Preferred Stock Index™ (1980-Present).

This preferred-stock composite takes the percentage changes of the discontinued Mitchell Preferred Stock Average and the discontinued S&P's preferred-stock studies and combines them with the Winans International Preferred Stock Index's to form a continuous price chart of preferred stocks.

Since 1900, preferred stocks have increased an average of 7.3% a year (non-war inflation adjusted return was 5.0%). The best annual return was 40.8% in 1986. The worst annual return was -22.5% in 1907. The 105-year average annual dividend yield was 6.4%. Preferreds had negative years 24.8% of the time, and back-to-back negative years 6.6% of the time.

If $1 had been invested in preferreds in December 1900, it would have been worth $1,028 in December 2005 (non-war inflation adjusted value was $82) (CHART 7).

PREFERREDS' PERFORMANCE VERSUS OTHER INCOME INVESTMENTS

All analysis should start with a review of long-term performance when comparing different investment mediums. Here are the facts from this 105-year study.

Common Stocks (S&P 500 Index and Extensions)

Common stocks have vastly outperformed all income investments in the past 105 years. With an average annual total return of 11.4%, common stocks reign as the best growth investment. However, with an average annual dividend of 4.5% they didn't come close to matching preferred stocks (6.4%) as an income-producing investment (CHART 8).

Corporate Bonds (Dow Jones Corporate Bond 20 Index and Extensions)

After 1900, corporate bonds have had an average annual return increase of 5.8% (non-war inflation adjusted return was 3.5%). The best annual return was 38.5% in 1982. The worst one was -13.9% in 1931. The 105-year average annual interest yield was 5.7%. Corporate bonds had negative years 21.0% of the time, plus back-to-back negative years 3.8% of the time. If $1 had been invested in corporate bonds in December 1900, it would have been worth $296 in December 2005 (non-war inflation adjusted value was $24) (CHART 9).

Although slightly more volatile, preferred stocks have vastly outperformed corporate bonds over the long term and proved to be a better inflation hedge for income investors.

Municipal Bonds (The Bond Buyer 20 Index and Extensions)

In the years since 1900, municipal bond average tax-free yields were 4.6%, while the yield adjusted for the current highest federal tax bracket was 6.2%. With an average dividend of 6.4%, preferreds actually stand "toe-to-toe" with muni bonds, one of the favorite income investments of wealthy Americans. While most municipal bonds have protections against default, preferred stocks usually offer better liquidity and lower transaction costs (CHART 10).

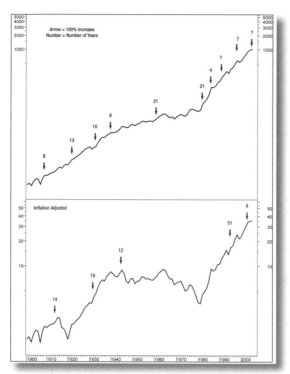

CHART 7—Preferred Stock Total and Inflation Adjusted Returns 1900-2005

Created in MetaStock from Equis International

CHART 8—Common Stock Total and Inflation Adjusted Returns 1900-2005

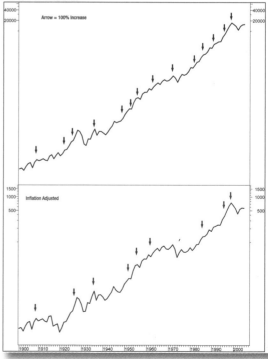

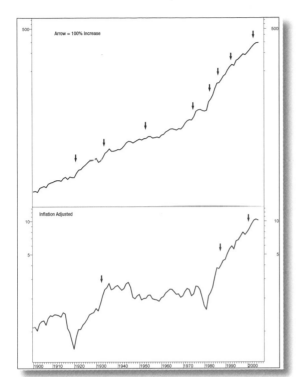

CHART 9–Corporate Bond Total
and Inflation Adjusted Returns
1900-2005

CHART 10–Municipal Bond Total
and Inflation Adjusted Returns
1900-2005

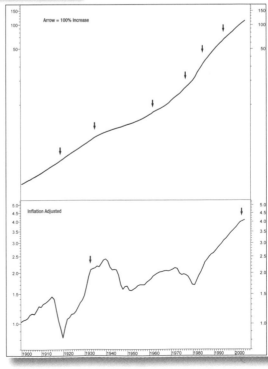

What the above studies plainly show is that preferred stocks are historically one of the best income investments. In addition to great performance, preferred stocks have several advantages and disadvantages that could affect their individual returns.

ADVANTAGES

Marginable

Many preferreds are marginable (i.e., used as collateral for brokerage house loans) and can provide the flexibility to take advantage of new investment opportunities without the commitment of new investment capital.

Exchange Listed

Because they are exchange-listed securities, they are great substitutes for medium to long-term bonds and can be purchased at most brokerage houses.

No Accrued Interest

In addition to investment and transaction costs, new bond purchasers have to pay the previous holder's interest owed up to the point of sale. The purchaser of preferred stocks doesn't owe accrued payments of any type and is subject to the same rules about ex-dividend dates as the holders of common stocks.

Another Way to Own Real Estate

Real Estate Investment Trust (REITs) and home building companies regularly issue preferred stocks that pay yields comparable to illiquid second trust deeds or rental properties.

Global Opportunities

Many foreign companies issue preferreds that trade in the U.S. and abroad.

DISADVANTAGES

Mutual Funds

There are very few choices in traditional preferred stock mutual funds, so small investors might have difficulty investing in these securities.

Listed Stock Options

Unfortunately, there are no listed stock options currently available on preferred stocks, which limits hedging opportunities.

Chapter 4

Winans International Preferred Stock Index™ (WIPSI™)

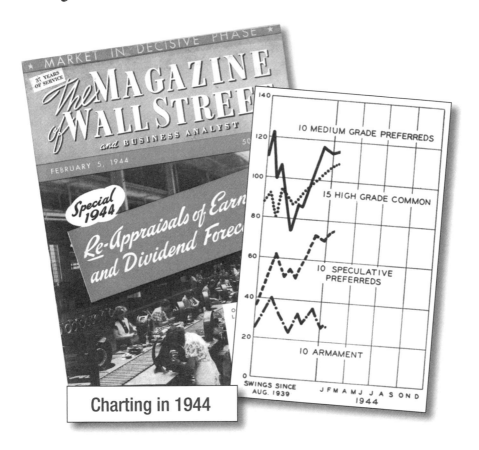

Charting in 1944

"Market analysis is based heavily on the movement of broad market averages."
TECHNICAL ANALYSIS OF THE FINANCIAL MARKETS, JOHN MURPHY, 1999

*"While preferred stocks rarely enjoy the same price gains as common stocks,
these shares also are not as vulnerable to sharp declines.
The average preferred stock fell only 3% in the past year
versus a 21% drop in the S&P 500."*
FORBES, NOVEMBER 18, 2002

The WIPSI™ is the first investment index devoted solely to tracking the price and yield of traditional preferred stocks from 1980 to present.

One might ask, "Why is it important to have an index for preferred stocks?" The simple answer is that people are increasingly being exposed to these securities by major newspapers and Web sites that list hundreds of individual preferred stocks daily. Investors need a way to broadly monitor these investments and to evaluate their past performance. After all, a common stock investor uses the S&P 500 Index or the Dow Jones Industrial Average to track the overall market. Why shouldn't the same investor be able to use an index to follow preferred stocks?

HISTORY

I initially realized there was a problem in 2003 when I began to add more preferred stocks to my portfolios to make up for the increasing shortage of exchange-listed corporate bonds. I had been tracking the various types of fixed-income investments (U.S. Treasury, municipal, corporate, etc.) and other equity-income investments (REITs, utilities, Master Limited Partnerships, etc.) through established indices; however when it came to preferred stocks, I was stymied and somewhat "flying blind" due to the lack of an index to help me follow price trends and historical valuations versus other types of income investments.

No one was offering a "pure" preferred stock index. In fact, the two associations that most investment analysts are members of, The Chartered Financial Analyst Institute and The Market Technicians Association, produce "think tank" type publications devoted to market and investment analysis. Surprisingly, I found very little research on preferred stocks—past or present.

The problem became more evident when I assisted *Forbes* magazine in compiling data for an article titled "Reaching for Yield" for the 2004 Special Summer Issue. The publication's reporter became frustrated because there was no way to show the long-term performance of preferred stocks or to compare them with other investments. In summary, the WIPSI is needed for several reasons:

- Many media sources have recently added "Preferred Stock" sections to their publications and Web sites, yet they do not list corresponding benchmarks for preferreds.
- Preferred stocks have been a part of Wall Street since its inception. In fact, most undergraduate and graduate textbooks devote space

to discussing the differences between common stocks, bonds, and preferred stocks. Neither Wall Street nor the financial textbooks are able to compare their relative investment performances without a preferred- stock index.

CURRENT COMPONENTS OF WIPSI (EVEN WEIGHTING)

COMPANY	SYMBOL
Alabama Power	ALP-N
Alcoa	AA-
Bear Stearns	BSC-E
Cleveland Electric Financial	CVE-U
Consolidated Edison	ED-A
Consumers Power	CMS-B
Travelers/Citibank	C-G
DuPont	DD-A
Duquesne Light	DQU-C
Equity Residential	EQR-D
Freddie Mac	FRE-K
Georgia Power	GPE-W
Lehman Brothers	LEH-C
HSBC Finance	HFC-B
Kansas City Southern	KSU-
MBNA	KRB-D
Merrill Lynch	MER-F
Monongahela Power	MPN-A
Niagara Mohawk	NMK-B
Pacific Gas & Electric	PCG-A
Pacific Enterprise	PET-A
PECO Energy	PE-A
Protective Life Capital	PL-A
Public Storage	PSA-V
So. Carolina E&G	SAC-
San Diego G&E	SDO-A
Torchmark	TMK-A
Virginia Power	VEL-A
Wisconsin Power	WIS-

SUPPLEMENTAL INFORMATION

Average Standard & Poor's Rating	BBB	
Industry Breakdown	Utilities	50%
	Financial Services	33%
	Industrial	7%
	Business Services	7%
Average Annual Revenues	$11.3 billion	
Year-end Dividend Cycle	December	60%
	November	23%
	October	17%

APPLICATIONS

The WIPSI™ has been configured to be used to construct charts and spread-sheet tables that can be used with the index's price, yield, total return, and supplemental data in several ways:

- **Charting**
  Price, yield, and total-return charts can be used to determine long- to short-term price trends, changes in long- to short-term trends, and overbought to oversold market conditions. Conventional technical tools, such as chart patterns, moving averages, and relative strength indicators, can be easily used on computer charting packages. The data are currently formatted for MetaStock and spreadsheet software. Daily charts and data can be downloaded from Global Financial Data (www.globalfinancialdata.com).
- **Yield Spreads**
  The yield data can be combined with yield data from other investments to make yield spreads for valuation comparisons over a long time frame.
- **Supplemental Information**
  Information on the index's average ratings, industry sector breakdown, dividend cycle, and other financial information is compiled annually.

For more details on the index's construction, data used, or weighting, please review "WIPSI Specifications" later in the book.

Chapter 5

Investment Analysis of Preferred Stocks

Preferred Stock Certificate
Baltimore and Ohio Railroad, 1875

"Values are determined roughly by the earnings available for dividends."
ABC OF STOCK SPECULATION, S.A. NELSON, 1903

*"One of the great strengths of technical analysis is
its adaptability to virtually any trading medium and time frame."*
TECHNICAL ANALYSIS OF THE FINANCIAL MARKETS, JOHN MURPHY, 1999

*"The terms and structures of traditional and hybrid preferred securities
are unfortunately complex, can vary significantly and are constantly evolving."*
FLAHERTY INVESTMENT RESEARCH REPORT, 2005

In investing, there are two basic types of analysis: technical and fundamental. Technical investment analysis focuses on the movement of security prices over time. Fundamental mainly deals with the relationship of various corporate financial figures to the investment's price in determining a valuation.

While both types of analysis are used in this book, the primary spotlight is on technical analysis because the economic forces that move the investment price in a certain direction are the same in the long term.

Have you heard the expression "A picture is worth 1,000 words"? Well, the pictures in this book are mainly charts of past investment prices. Charts are the most effective tools for depicting historical investment trends. When coupled with some of the tools discussed later, they are great resources for analyzing investments.

In looking at the following examples of the WIPSI™ (CHART 11, TABLE 4), which is easier to use in identifying price trends: the price chart or the raw data in a column of numbers? On the vertical scale is the price of the index and the horizontal scale is time; any point on the chart represents the price of the index at a given time (bar charts at the bottom of a price chart typically represent the volume traded at a given period of time). Clearly, the chart is a more effective way to analyze the WIPSI's price history.

The critics of technical analysis will tell you that investment prices don't trend and move randomly through time. Their unrealistic answer to investing is to "buy all the time." As you study the following pages, it will become obvious that investment prices do trend over long periods of time.

Essentially, the varied emotions, such as fear and greed, that people have about money and investing haven't changed much over time, so their actions typically resemble those of previous investors.

It should also be noted that although numerous technical studies could have been done, the focus was on basic indicators that can be easily used by investors from various sources at little or no charge. (See the "Preferred Stock Information" section in the back of the book for a list of information sources.)

CHART 11–WIPSI™ (Price)
1980-Present

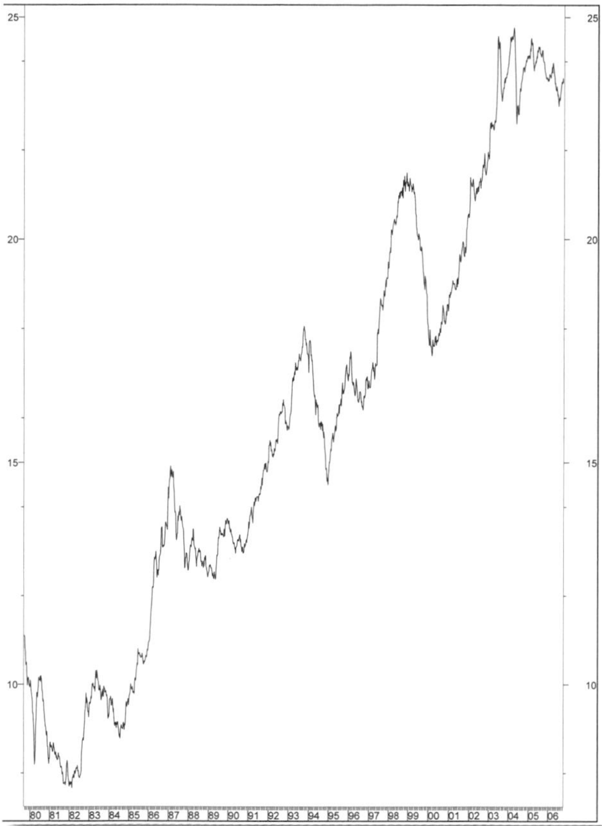

Created in MetaStock from Equis International

TABLE 4–WIPSI
Price and Year-to-Year
Change
1981-2005

Year-end	Index Value	Yr to Yr % Change
1980	8.58	
1981	7.99	-6.9%
1982	9.62	20.4%
1983	9.63	0.1%
1984	9.88	2.6%
1985	11.19	13.3%
1986	14.57	30.2%
1987	12.93	-11.3%
1988	12.81	-0.9%
1989	14.04	9.6%
1990	13.76	-2.0%
1991	15.46	12.4%
1992	16.2	4.8%
1993	17.75	9.6%
1994	14.84	-16.4%
1995	17.19	15.8%
1996	17.17	-0.1%
1997	19.64	14.4%
1998	21.49	9.4%
1999	18.34	-14.7%
2000	18.71	2.0%
2001	20.82	11.3%
2002	22.19	6.6%
2003	24.34	9.7%
2004	24.41	0.3%
2005	23.78	-2.6%

BASIC ANALYSIS OF THE
WINANS INTERNATIONAL PREFERRED STOCK INDEX™ (WIPSI™)

Because this is a new index, the aim of the analysis was limited to determining if conventional analysis would work for identifying changes in the long-term investment trends of preferred stocks. One of the most useful and easy-to-follow indicators for trend analysis of market indices is the 200-day simple moving average (CHART 12).

The general interpretation of this indicator is:
- **Uptrend (i.e., Bullish)**
    If the price of the index is above the moving average.
- **Downtrend (i.e., Bearish)**
    If the price of the index is below the moving average.
- **Change of the Trend's Direction**
    If the price of the index penetrates the moving average.

Data Examined

As can be seen in CHARTS 13-17 from 1980-2005, there were eight signals indicating the beginning of an uptrend and seven forecasting the start of a downtrend. This indicator was accurate 87% of the time. The index had an average advance of 21.1% over 100 weeks from uptrend signals and an average decline of 5.3% during 58 weeks from downtrend signs.

This information is useful because it helps identify good times to be an investor in preferred stocks and periods when investors should be more cautious. It also indicates opportune times to be buying new investments or selling unwanted holdings.

Moving Average Analysis

As a final note, no indicator, including the 200-day moving average, should be used alone. Remember that this indicator was wrong 13% of the time and other types of investment analysis can be useful to "filter" bad signals.

A more extensive analysis on the WIPSI that list many other indicators successfully used over a 25-year time frame is presented later in the book.

CHART 12—WIPSI Moving Average Analysis (40-Week)
1981-2005

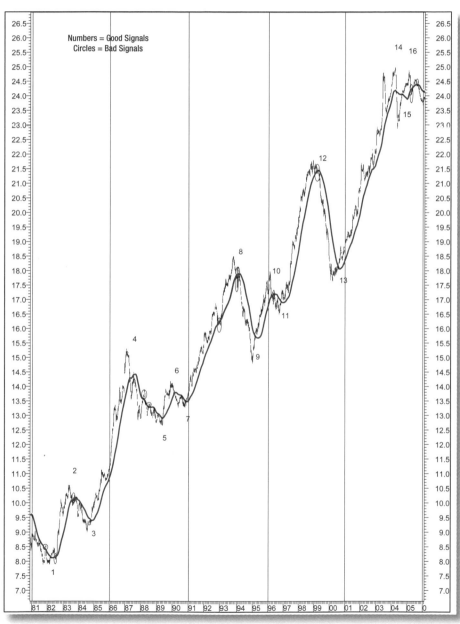

Created in MetaStock from Equis International

CHART 13–WIPSI Moving Average Analysis (40-Week)
1981-1985

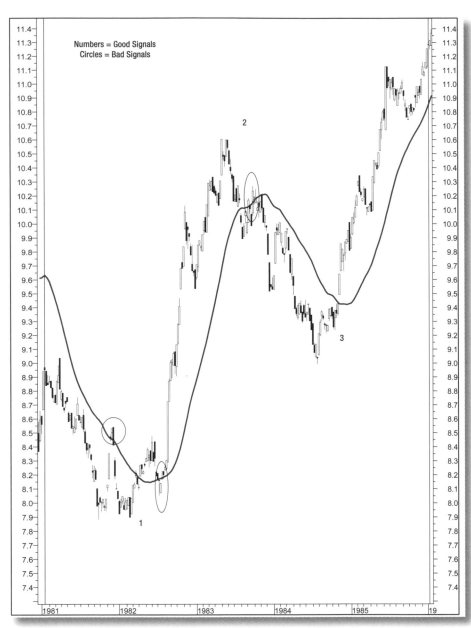

Created in MetaStock from Equis International

CHART 14–WIPSI Moving Average Analysis (40-Week)
1986-1990

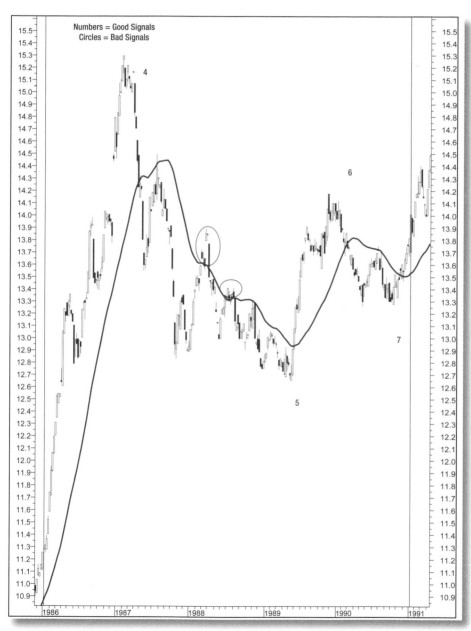

Created in MetaStock from Equis International

CHART 15–WIPSI Moving Average Analysis (40-Week)
1991-1995

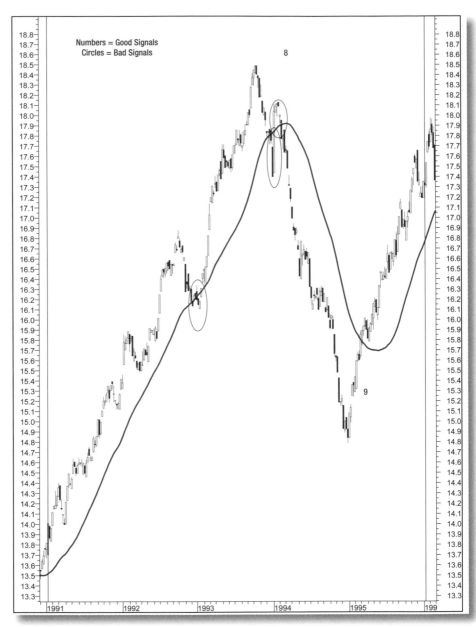

Numbers = Good Signals
Circles = Bad Signals

CHART 16–WIPSI Moving Average Analysis (40-Week)
1996-2000

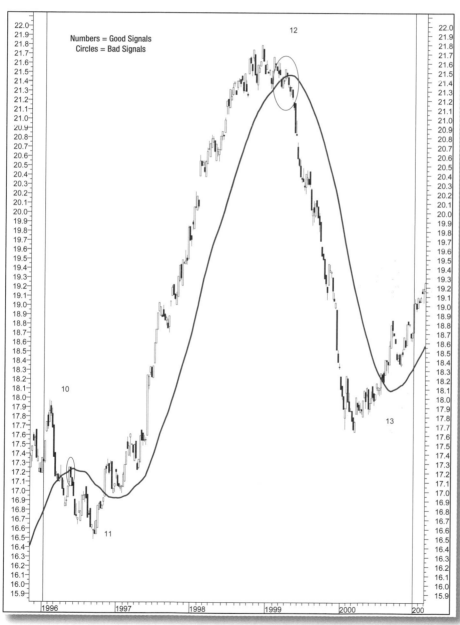

CHART 17—WIPSI Moving Average Analysis (40-Week)
2001-2005

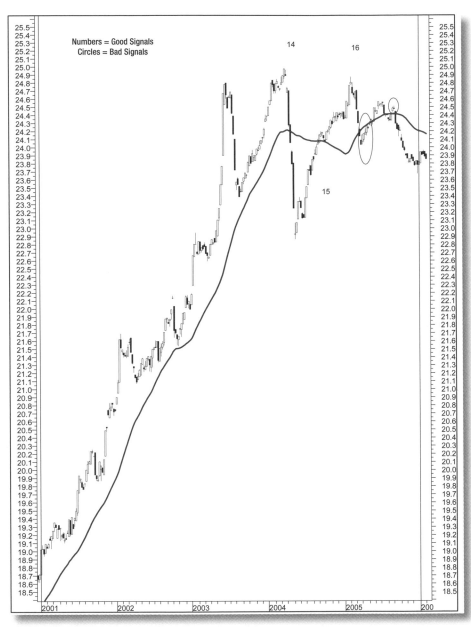

Numbers = Good Signals
Circles = Bad Signals

BASIC ANALYSIS OF INDIVIDUAL PREFERRED STOCKS

The purpose of this analysis was to decide if common technical approaches would work in identifying long-term changes in the trends of the preferred stocks selected. As in the case of the WIPSI™, this is uncharted territory that has not been extensively tested. An eight-year period (1998-2005) was picked, using weekly data on prices and volume (the bottom scale on each chart), because most preferred stocks have limited "lifetimes."

Selection Process

Individual preferred stocks are used in this analysis.

Three traditional (or straight), nonconvertible preferred stocks were selected for the following reasons:

- These stocks display the trading characteristics of most preferred stocks that actively trade. To make comparisons to the WIPSI meaningful, the research was directed at straight preferred stocks.
- They are from industries that have historically issued preferred stocks (i.e., Alcoa–manufacturing, Consolidated Edison–utility, Merrill Lynch–finance) and are components of the WIPSI.
- They have continuously traded since 1998.
- They have been given high ratings by Standard & Poor's (BBB or higher).

Data Filtering Analysis

Prior to analyzing the investment merits of an individual preferred stock, its price and volume data have to be carefully screened for inaccuracies caused by periodic illiquidity. It should also be noted that price gaps caused by quarterly dividends need to be carefully evaluated, because they can cause false signals on technical indicators.

Fundamental and Ratings Analysis

Similar to bond analysis, reviewing the issuer's fundamentals and ratings is useful in the selection process of new preferred stock investments, as well as confirming other research. Using independent research companies, such as Valueline, an investor has a low-cost, effective way to conduct fundamental analysis.

In TABLE 5 is a fundamental analysis checklist to evaluate the financial strength of the companies using Valueline's research. An investment in a company with a significant number of negative factors is usually removed from the portfolio.

TABLE 6 shows how to compare the S&P ratings of corporate bonds and preferred stock.

TABLE 5—Fundamental Analysis Checklist

Corporate Bond and Preferred Stock Negative Factors
MAJOR

Private Company	(no financial information)
Common Stock Price	Within 10% of 52-week low
Common Stock Price	Below $3.00 per share
Earnings	Three years of losses out of of last five years
Cashflow	Three years of losses out of of last five years
Earnings	Big losses in last two years
Cashflow	Big losses in last two years
Earnings	Losses expected this year
Cashflow	Losses expected this year
Debt to Capital Ratio	More than 75%
Shares Outstanding	High levels of dilution
Valueline Safety Rating	4 or 5
Valueline Financial Strength	Less than B
Negative Accounting Notes and Other Concerns	

MINOR

Revenue	Reduction expected this year
Earnings	Reduction expected this year
Cashflow	Reduction expected this year
Common Dividends	Reduction expected this year
Operating Margin	Less than 7%
Long-term Debt vs Equity	10% increase in debt and reduction in equity
Common Dividend Payout Ratio	Greater than 100%
Revenue	Less than $500 million
Valueline Earnings Predictability	Less than 60
S&P Rating	Lowered

TABLE 6–S&P Corporate Rating Interpretations

Common Stock	Preferreds/ Bonds	General Interpretation
A+	AAA+	Risk Free
	AAA	
	AAA-	
A	AA+	
	AA	
	AA-	
	A+	
	A	
A-	A-	Investment Grade ↑
B+	BBB+	
	BBB	
	BBB-	
B	BB+	
	BB	Medium Grade
	BB-	
B-	B+	
	B	
	NR	"Junk" Rated ↓
	B-	
C+	CCC+	
	CCC	
	CCC-	
C	CC+	
	CC	
	CC-	
C-	C+	
	C	
	C-	
D	D	Default

Moving Average Analysis

One of the most useful and easy-to-follow indicators for trend analysis of individual investments is the 200-day moving average (also known as 40-week moving average). The general interpretation of the indicator is:

- It's an uptrend (i.e., bullish) if the price of the index is above the moving average.
- Things are in a downtrend (i.e., bearish) if the price of the index is below the moving average.
- And there is a change under way in the trend's direction if the price of the index penetrates the moving average.

After a time period for a moving average is chosen, such as 200 days, then the right type of moving average should be selected. Investors usually use simple (or non-weighted), time-weighted, or exponentially calculated moving averages in investment analysis. A review of the different types of 200-day moving averages on CHARTS 18-20 showed that of the 26 false signs that were triggered by only one or two moving average types, just one of the "bad signals" was from the simple moving average; it proved that the 200-day simple moving average is the most reliable type of indicator for this analysis.

Compare CHARTS 21-23 of the individual preferred stocks listed above with CHART 24 of the WIPSI. If you look closely, you'll probably notice that all the charts look similar and are useful in confirming buy or sell signals.

For example, if an investor had followed the bearish signals of the WIPSI, as well as those of the three individual charts in 1999, he or she would have been able to avoid a serious correction that followed. In 2000, strong buy signals were given, which preceded powerful, four-year-long rallies in the WIPSI and preferred stocks.

The proof's in the pudding: A great synergy can be produced by blending together an analysis of a market index with individual securities.

As with the analysis on the WIPSI, no indicator should be used alone. A more extensive analysis that lists many other indicators successfully used on these stocks is presented later in this book.

CHART 18–Preferred Stock Moving Averages Analysis
Alcoa pf A (40-Week, Incorrect Crossings)
1998-2005

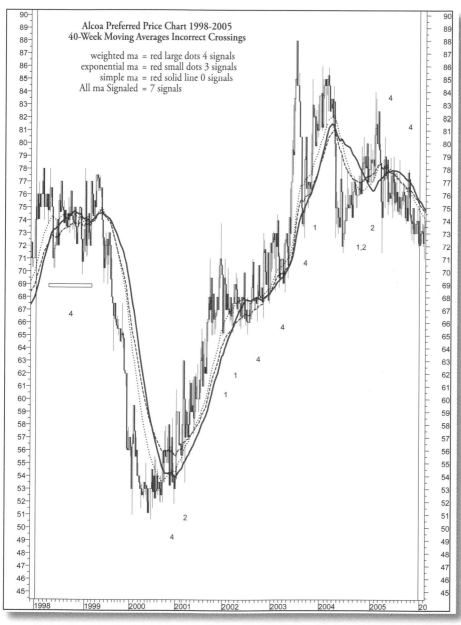

Alcoa Preferred Price Chart 1998-2005
40-Week Moving Averages Incorrect Crossings

weighted ma = red large dots 4 signals
exponential ma = red small dots 3 signals
simple ma = red solid line 0 signals
All ma Signaled = 7 signals

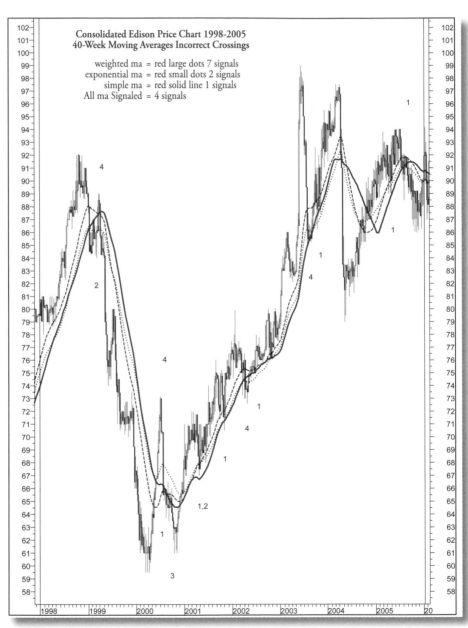

CHART 19–Preferred Stock Moving Averages Analysis
Consolidated Edison pf A (40-Week, Incorrect Crossings)
1998-2005

Consolidated Edison Price Chart 1998-2005
40-Week Moving Averages Incorrect Crossings

weighted ma = red large dots 7 signals
exponential ma = red small dots 2 signals
simple ma = red solid line 1 signals
All ma Signaled = 4 signals

Created in MetaStock from Equis International

CHART 20–Preferred Stock Moving Averages Analysis
Merrill Lynch pf B (40-Week, Incorrect Crossings)
1998-2005

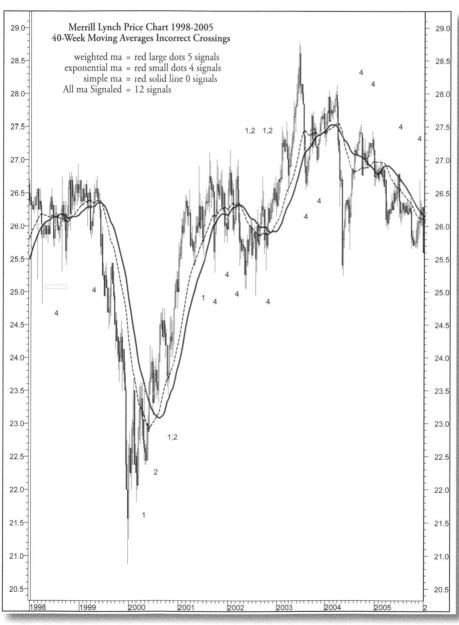

Merrill Lynch Price Chart 1998-2005
40-Week Moving Averages Incorrect Crossings

weighted ma = red large dots 5 signals
exponential ma = red small dots 4 signals
simple ma = red solid line 0 signals
All ma Signaled = 12 signals

Created in MetaStock from Equis International

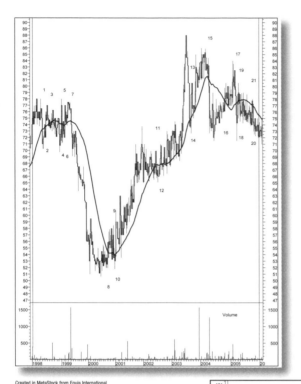

CHART 21–Preferred Stock
Moving Average Analysis
Alcoa pf A (40-Week)
1998-2005

Created in MetaStock from Equis International

CHART 22–Preferred Stock
Moving Average Analysis
Consolidated Edison pf A
(40-Week)
1998-2005

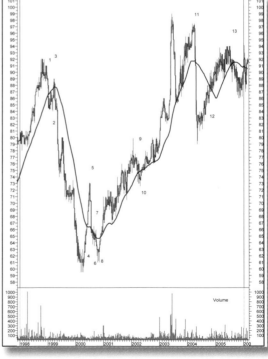

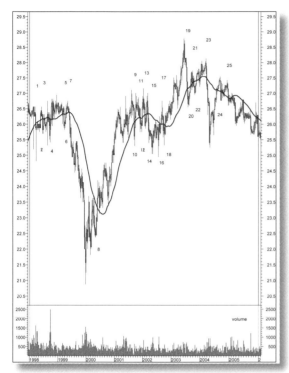

CHART 23–Preferred Stock
Moving Average Analysis
Merrill Lynch pf B (40-Week)
1998-2005

CHART 24–WIPSI™
Moving Average Analysis
(40-Week)
1998-2005

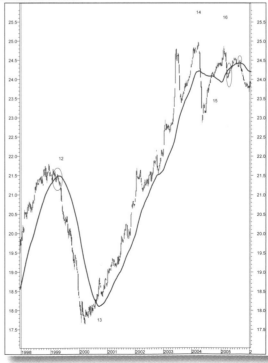

Chapter 6

Portfolio Management: Bringing It All Together

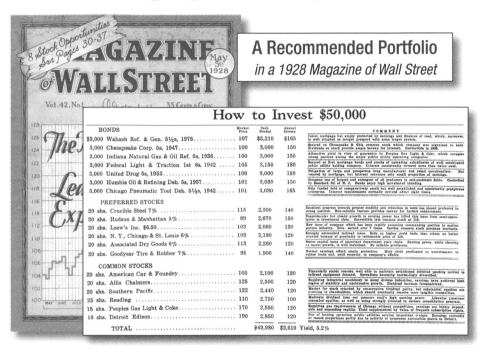

A Recommended Portfolio
in a 1928 Magazine of Wall Street

How to Invest $50,000

	Market Price	Cash Needed	Annual Income	COMMENT
BONDS				
$3,000 Wabash Ref. & Gen. 5½s, 1975	107	$3,210	$165	Junior mortgage but amply protected by earnings and finances of road, which, moreover, is well situated as merger prospect with some larger system.
3,000 Chesapeake Corp. 5s, 1947	100	3,000	150	Secured on Chesapeake & Ohio common stock which company was organized to hold. Dividends on stock provide ample leeway for interest. Convertible in 1932.
3,000 Indiana Natural Gas & Oil Ref. 5s, 1936	100	3,000	150	Attractive yield in view of guarantee by Peoples Gas Light & Coke, which occupies strong position among the major public utility operating companies.
3,000 Federal Light & Traction 1st 6s, 1942	105	3,150	180	Secured on first mortgage bonds and stocks of operating subsidiaries of well established public utility holding company. Interest consistently covered more than twice over.
3,000 United Drug 5s, 1953	100	3,000	150	Obligation of large and prosperous drug manufacturer and retail merchandiser. Not secured by mortgage, but interest consumes only small proportion of earnings.
3,000 Humble Oil & Refining Deb. 5s, 1937	101	3,030	150	Company one of largest and strongest of oil producers in mid-continent fields. Controlled by Standard Oil of N. J. Bonds enjoy high investment standing.
3,000 Chicago Pneumatic Tool Deb. 5½s, 1942	101	3,030	165	Only funded debt of comparatively small but well established and consistently prosperous enterprise. Interest requirements normally covered about eight times.
PREFERRED STOCKS				
20 shs. Crucible Steel 7%	115	2,300	140	Excellent progress towards greater stability and reduction in costs has placed preferred in strong position. Non-callable feature provides leeway for further enhancement.
30 shs. Hudson & Manhattan 5%	89	2,670	150	Unspectacular but steady growth in earning power has lifted this issue from semi-speculative to investment class. Convertible into common stock at 210.
20 shs. Loew's Inc. $6.50	103	2,060	130	New issue of company which has been rapidly assuming commanding position in motion picture industry. Divs. earned over 7 times. Carries common stock purchase warrants.
20 shs. N. Y., Chicago & St. Louis 6%	109	2,180	120	Strongly entrenched railroad issue. Sells on higher yield basis than others no better situated because of proximity to redeemable price of 110.
20 shs. Associated Dry Goods 6%	113	2,260	120	Senior capital issue of important department store chain. Earning power, while showing no recent growth, is well stabilized. No callable provisions.
20 shs. Goodyear Tire & Rubber 7%	95	1,900	140	Normal earnings afford ample protection. High yield predicated on uncertlement in rubber trade and, until recently, in company's affairs.
COMMON STOCKS				
20 shs. American Car & Foundry	105	2,100	120	Financially stable concern, well able to maintain established dividend pending revival in railroad equipment demand. Operations becoming increasingly diversified.
20 shs. Allis Chalmers	125	2,500	120	Supplying industrial machinery to many diverse industries, earnings have achieved high degree of stability and unobtrusive growth. Dividend increase foreshadowed.
20 shs. Southern Pacific	122	2,440	120	Market for stock retarded by conservative dividend policy, but substantial equities are accruing to shareholders, which should eventually receive more tangible recognition.
25 shs. Reading	110	2,750	100	Moderate dividend does not measure road's high earning power. Likewise possesses concealed equities, as well as being strongly situated in eastern consolidation program.
15 shs. Peoples Gas Light & Coke	170	2,550	120	Supplying gas requirements of Chicago without competition, earnings are highly dependable and expanding rapidly. Yield supplemented by value of frequent subscription rights.
15 shs. Detroit Edison	190	2,850	120	One of leading operating public utilities serving important centers. Earnings currently at record proportions partly due to activity of numerous automobile plants in Detroit.
TOTAL		$49,980	$2,610	Yield, 5.2%

*"If the bond market starts to diverge from the stock market, a warning is being given—
the more serious the divergence, the more important the warning...
the days of following only one market are long gone."*
INTERMARKET TECHNICAL ANALYSIS, MURPHY, 1991

*"All the market knowledge in the world will be useless without the ability
to put this knowledge into action by mastering our emotions."*
INVESTMENT PSYCHOLOGY EXPLAINED, PRING, 1993

*"Retirement shortfalls from the stock market downturn in recent years
and demographic trends are creating a longer term yearning for yield
within the financial markets."*
BARRON'S, APRIL 14, 2005

Successful investing requires an investor to "separate the forest from the trees." This is especially true when you're working on incorporating preferreds into a portfolio, also known as portfolio or investment management.

SETTING A REALISTIC PERFORMANCE GOAL

A good game plan will more than likely lead to good results. Begin by setting up realistic performance goals based on historical facts.

How can you do this? The art and science of successful investing requires an understanding of history, statistics, and common sense. A solid goal will blend together ideas from these disciplines. Your performance goal will be the base your financial decisions will rest on over the next five years. Setting and adhering to a realistic goal could turn you into a successful investor instead of someone who, for instance, randomly puts in buy and sell orders based on tips they may have heard at a dinner party. Goals offer protection: With them, you can continue to grow your portfolio; without them, you may fall prey to the "easy money" psychology generated by a bull market or the unbridled fear that can be unleashed on investors by a bear market.

TABLE 7 gives projected results based on 15-year historical returns from established investment indices (S&P 500, Dow Jones Corporate 20 Bond Index). By using the historical returns of a longer time period to set goals for shorter schedules, you'll improve the chances of achieving your desired results. For example, an investor who needs all profits to be in the form of income or has a very low tolerance for uncertainty will probably decide to have most of his or her funds invested in income investments such as corporate bonds and preferred stocks. Based on historical returns, the investor has a 95% chance of obtaining a cumulative return of 38% over five years (i.e., 7.6% annualized).

Remember, there are going to be bad years. Investors who stay on track have a good chance of realizing their long-term goals.

TABLE 7–5 Year Portfolio Performance and Asset Allocation Projections

5 Year Portfolio Performance Goal & Asset Allocation Projections   December, 2005

15 Year Total Annual Returns (%):

	Cumulative:	Annual:	Calculation:	Success Probabilites:	Goal:
S&P 500 Index	18.6%	10.6%	14.6%	80.0%	11.7%
Dow Jones Corporate 20	7.6%	11.5%	9.6%	95.0%	9.1%

Stock Amount	Stock Asset Allocation	Bond Amount	Bond Asset Allocation	Portfolio Goal	Portfolio Success Probabilities	Capital Gains $	Income $	Average Annual Return $
$500,000	100%	$0	0%	11.7%	80%	$48,400	$10,000	$58,400
$0.00	0%	$500,000	100%	9.1%	95%	$0	$45,363	$45,363

EXECUTING THE INVESTMENT GAME PLAN

Once the goal and asset allocation have been set, the job of constructing the portfolio begins. In previous sections, various investment analysis indicators were reviewed to help an investor identify investment candidates and reasonable price levels for purchases of preferred stocks. Because income investments can vary in availability and valuation, patience is required to build an income portfolio. In general, it can take up to 90 days to finish the portfolio construction process. And it is also important to remember that it could take up to six months to receive any income from your investments.

The first year of owning an income portfolio is like building a new apartment building.

- You have to pay to construct the building before rental income is received.

  (i.e., transaction costs, accrued interest, etc.)

- It takes time to find good tenants, so the building is usually not 100% occupied when it's completed.

  (i.e., availability of income investments)

- Tenants move in at different times, so they will pay rent on different schedules and amounts based on their rental agreements.

  (i.e., income investments pay different amounts of interest and dividends at various times)

Here's a good tip. The performance clock starts ticking after the portfolio construction phase. Don't compare the returns of an income portfolio to a goal or market index until at least one year after the portfolio is "built."

MONITORING THE PORTFOLIO

A lot of information is needed to properly monitor a portfolio. Unfortunately, many investors are being overloaded with information from various sources. As mentioned earlier, an income investor should not use data solely provided by brokerage houses in evaluating investments. Instead, you'll need to get additional information from other sources (see list in back of book) to properly evaluate the health and progress of your income portfolio.

PORTFOLIO PERFORMANCE

These are the reports I use to check the performance of income investments. One is for bonds, while the other covers income stocks, such as preferred stocks, Real Estate Investment Trusts, and energy partnerships (Exhibit 6).

This report is very useful and provides information typically not available in brokerage statements. Here are some sets of data that are great for reviewing the overall performance of this income portfolio:

Exhibit 6–Performance Report
Corporate Bonds

Description	Market Value	Par Value	Annual Yield %	Year to Date Change %	Cumulative Change $	Cumulative Income
Corporate Bonds						
CORPORATE BOND 7.5% 02/15/11	$25,470	$25,000	7.5%	-0.2%	$465	$1,808
CORPORATE BOND 7.2% 07/15/08	$15,559	$25,000	7.1%	-1.9%	$60	$7,042
CORPORATE BOND 7.75% 03/01/07	$6,053	$6,000	7.5%	-1.9%	($113)	$2,744
CORPORATE BOND 9.05% 11/15/11	$26,013	$24,000	8.1%	-2.1%	($843)	$4,630
CORPORATE BOND 7.875% 07/15/13	$11,220	$12,000	7.9%	-9.2%	($766)	$7,826
CORPORATE BOND 7.625% 5/15/0	$25,563	$25,000	7.3%	-2.0%	($723)	$7,458
CORPORATE BOND 7.75% 02/1/10	$15,000	$15,000	7.7%	-4.3%	($103)	$4,255
CORPORATE BOND 9.375% 06/01/11	$15,675	$15,000	9.1%	-0.2%	$259	$4,369
CORPORATE BOND 8.75% 07/15/07	$21,394	$21,000	8.2%	-2.0%	($927)	$15,593
CORPORATE BOND 8.25% 12/15/11	$24,750	$25,000	8.3%	2.1%	($5)	$1,712
CORPORATE BOND 10.75% 10/15/06	$8,150	$10,000	10.5%	-19.3%	($2,136)	$1,496
CORPORATE BOND 6.5% 08/15/10	$23,500	$25,000	6.7%	-1.8%	($755)	$1,345
CORPORATE BOND 7.75% 03/15/13	$45,360	$48,000	7.4%	-3.4%	($4,975)	$5,668
CORPORATE BOND 7% 05/01/12	$15,525	$15,000	6.9%	-1.4%	$380	$3,153
CORPORATE BOND 6.85% 06/01/08	$9,135	$9,000	7.1%	-1.5%	$494	$2,809
CORPORATE BOND 6.0% 01/04/14	$28,050	$30,000	6.9%	-6.5%	$1,940	$5,701
Corporate Bonds Subtotal	**$326,416**	**$330,000**	**7.8%**	**-2.9%**	**($7,747)**	**$74,608**

Income Stocks

Description	Shares	Market Value	Average Div. Yield %	Year to Date Change %	Cumulative Change $	Cumulative Income $
Equity Income						
COMMON STOCK	865	$26,132	7.9%	2.9%	$1,094	$1,603
PREFERRED STOCK 8.7%	887	$24,295	7.1%	0.3%	($2,907)	$3,647
PREFERRED STOCK 8.00%	949	$24,627	7.5%	-0.9%	($579)	$3,588
PREFERRED STOCK 8.6%	956	$24,311	8.2%	-3.6%	$897	$1,064
COMMON STOCK	221	$9,724	8.0%	14.3%	$2,143	$1,700
PREFERRED STOCK 8.765%	838	$21,646	7.9%	0.4%	($1,754)	$3,485
PREFERRED STOCK 8.3%	848	$22,345	7.3%	-30.5%	($2,994)	$2,934
PREFERRED STOCK 8.125%	919	$23,591	7.4%	-1.9%	($1,710)	$4,953
PREFERRED STOCK 7.25%	284	$7,214	6.7%	-0.5%	($414)	$1,738
COMMON STOCK	276	$9,748	5.2%	-19.0%	($2,896)	$535
PREFERRED STOCK 8%	282	$26,085	10.1%	4.3%	$1,066	$56
PREFERRED STOCK 9%	950	$24,064	8.4%	0.3%	($1,425)	$5,675
COMMON STOCK	1,335	$21,654	8.4%	0.2%	($2,255)	$1,618
Equity Income Subtotal		**$265,433**	**7.7%**	**-3.8%**	**($13,526)**	**$32,596**

Market Value versus Par (Maturity) Value

In comparing the market value to the par value you will notice that the bond holdings are currently worth more at maturity than if they were liquidated today ($326,416 versus $330,000). Remember that par value is a legal obligation that the issuer owes the holder of these bonds at maturity, so market value is relevant only if you need instant cash.

Annual Yield versus Year to Date Price Change

The "Annual Yield" and "Average Dividend Yield %" calculation (projected interest or dividends for the year/cost basis) shows the percentage earned on the income paid this year without the income being reinvested as reported by the yield to maturity statistic. The "Year to Date Price Change" measures the change in the price of an investment for the current year. In this example, the bond investments have declined (2.9%) and the income stocks have fallen (3.8%) so far during the year. One way to interpret this is that the investments have caused a loss within the portfolio. And, if the prices do not decline any further, the total return of the portfolio will be positive after all income is collected by the end of the year (7.8% for bonds and 7.7% for the income stocks).

A common mistake is to compare an income investment's annual price change to a market benchmark (such as the WIPSI or the Dow Jones Corporate Bond Average) without including the investment's estimated income. Such an error will cause the total annual performance of the investment to be underestimated.

Cumulative Change in Price versus Cumulative Income Received

To measure how an investment has performed since being purchased, cumulative returns should be analyzed. Since the investments in this portfolio have been purchased, they have declined ($7,747 for bonds; $13,526 for income investments) in value. And on the positive side, these investments have produced a large amount of income ($74,608 for bonds; $32,596 for income investments). In the final analysis, the investments as a group have been profitable to own.

Please keep in mind that some equity income investments have dividend yields that can fluctuate over time, so the "Dividend Yield %" is an estimate based on the average of the last two years of dividend payments.

In summary, there are many ways to evaluate the performance of an income portfolio. Although each method should be reviewed, it is more important for investors with long time horizons to review the cumulative returns annually against five-year performance goals they have set than to compare their annualized returns with market benchmarks every quarter.

PORTFOLIO HEALTH AND QUALITY

Exhibit 7 is a copy of a report I use to monitor an income portfolio's overall strength. It answers some basic questions.

- How is the overall long-term performance in light of the goal previously established?
- Is the portfolio's asset allocation or investment mix the same as set in the five-year investment strategy?
- Is the portfolio properly diversified by year of maturity, investment type (government debt, corporate bond, preferred stock, etc.) and agency ratings?

Cumulative Return

Cumulative return is an effective way to evaluate the performance of an income portfolio. This portfolio is in good shape: It's produced a 23% total return (8% annually) over the past three years. That puts it ahead of its five-year goal, as well as the market benchmark that was used. Remember that all deposits and withdrawals can affect the performance figures and need to be checked.

Asset Allocation and Five-Year Goal

You can see that this portfolio is set up as a 100% income portfolio with a five-year annual performance goal of 7%.

Maturity Schedule

This allows an investor to track when various types of income investments will be maturing (or called early) each year and to plan future investments. This portfolio has 37 individual positions with an average maturity year of 2012, with 19% of the portfolio's corporate and real estate income holdings coming due over the next two years. Also, 35% of the entire portfolio is callable—the investments could be called within the current year. Notice that investments without a due date such as preferreds are treated like long-term holdings placed at 10 years (twice

Exhibit 7–Portfolio Statisitics Summary

Portfolio Statistics Summary (Income Investments):

Portfolio Performance (Year-End):

Reporting Period (# of Years)	Cumulative	Cumulative Annual	Performance Goal	Market Benchmark Average
3	23%	8%	7%	4%

Asset Allocation:

Growth Investments	Income Investments	A. Allocation Changes
0%	100%	None

Portfolio Value & Investment Type:

Market Value	Number of Positions		Value	Portfolio Breakdown	Annual Yield	Year to Date Price Change
$977,710	37	Bond:	$641,187	76%	7.8%	-2.9%
		Equity Income:	$199,454	24%	7.7%	-3.8%

Maturity & Ratings:

Average Maturity 2012	Currently Callable	Average S&P Equivalent Rating	Financial Condition
	35%	BB	None

Equity Income Breakdown:

	Preferred Stock	Common Stock	Real Estate Inv. Trust	Listed Partnership
% of Port Value	$126,910	6% $51,475	1% $10,774	1% $10,295

Maturity Schedule:

	2006	2007	2008	2009	2010	2011	2012	2013	2014	2015	2016
Maturity Value	$0	$27,000	$134,600	$50,000	$40,000	$114,000	$130,000	$110,000	$30,000	$0	$231,523
% of Income	0%	3%	16%	6%	5%	13%	15%	13%	3%	0%	27%
Corporate Bd	$0	$27,000	$59,000	$0	$40,000	$114,000	$90,000	$110,000	$30,000	$0	$0
Equity Income	$0	$0	$0	$0	$0	$0	$0	$0	$0	$0	$231,523
Municipal Bd	$0	$0	$0	$0	$0	$0	$40,000	$0	$0	$0	$0
Treasury Bd	$0	$0	$0	$0	$0	$0	$0	$0	$0	$0	$0
Real Estate TD	$0	$0	$75,600	$50,000	$0	$0	$0	$0	$0	$0	$0

Industry Sectors:

	Finance	Health	Retail	Service	Technology	Industrial	Staple	Energy	Utility	Real Estate
% of Portfolio	9%	0%	1%	15%	9%	36%	14%	2%	2%	12%
Position Number	3	0	1	4	3	9	5	1	1	4
Market Value	$58,219	$0	$9,000	$100,000	$60,000	$245,069	$96,829	$10,295	$15,000	$82,111

the length of the performance goal time frame).

Equity Investment Breakdown

This shows how the income portfolio is invested. The portfolio consists of 76% of investments in bonds and 24% in equity income securities (15% preferred stocks and 8% in other investments).

Industry Breakdown

This shows how much exposure the portfolio has by industry group. Notice that the portfolio has high exposure to industrial companies and none to healthcare companies. Future investments in industrial companies should be thought through carefully.

Other Facts

Investors should also monitor changes in independent agency ratings, as well as any deterioration in the fundamentals of the corporations that issued the securities, whether or not they are bonds or preferreds.

Keep in mind that following a portfolio should involve more than just checking the market value from a brokerage statement or Web site. Recommendation—do your homework when the investment markets are not open; it's a quiet time to get things done!

REBALANCING THE PORTFOLIO

I've always thought that investment portfolios are like trees. After all, they are constantly changing their sizes and shapes. In both cases, growth is considered healthy. And there are times when trees and portfolios need to be pruned to enhance future growth.

In the case of investment portfolios, "pruning" or periodic rebalancing involves reinvesting the proceeds of investments that have matured or sold into new investments that will better diversify your portfolio. For example, what if one of your investments is from a company whose finances have deteriorated? Or what about a firm that is no longer publicly traded? Are you prepared to keep such an investment, even though financial information about it may become harder to obtain? Even if either of these companies is still paying interest and dividends, you might benefit in the long term by selling your investment and putting your proceeds into a stronger, publicly traded firm.

Although rebalancing is usually performed quarterly, an investor must always keep an eye open for investments that are suffering from volatile price declines. Because investment price usually leads business developments, it is wise to be defensive and consider removing these investments from an income portfolio. With income investing, it is better to be safe than sorry.

Rebalancing is often done for tax reasons. If you need capital losses to offset capital gains, then investments showing a loss can be sold, while new investments are bought immediately. This is usually called a tax swap.

Does successful investing take time and continued work? Absolutely! And the best investors immerse themselves in the discipline and knowledge that's necessary to "stay the course" in both bull and bear markets.

Due to the time and knowledge required, many investors have elected to retain the services of a "money manager" or investment advisor to oversee the investment process. However, the investor still needs to be actively involved in the important process of setting a realistic goal and periodically reviewing the portfolio with the money manager.

Chapter 7

Preferred Practical Tips

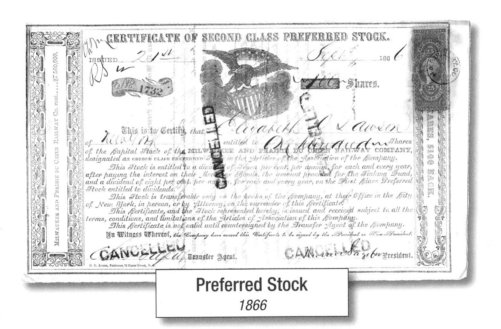

Preferred Stock
1866

*"Do not buy a convertible preferred unless
you think that the common stock of the company
is an attractive medium of speculation."*
MAKING MONEY IN STOCK TRADING, BARRON'S, 1943

*"Existing preferreds become less attractive when rates rise,
but since corporate borrowing costs are higher they're less likely to be called."*
THE WALL STREET JOURNAL, AUGUST 6, 2006

*"Dividend players have a much higher tolerance for price fluctuation,
but they don't have much tolerance for dividend cuts."*
THE WALL STREET JOURNAL, SEPTEMBER 19, 2006

There are practical issues involving all investments that only experience teaches most investors. Listed below are some things investors will need to know to maximize the benefits of using preferred stocks properly in their portfolios.

How and Where to Buy Preferred Stocks

Because they are listed on major stock exchanges in the U.S. and abroad, preferreds can be bought in the same manner as other stocks. Remember, because many of these stocks don't trade every day, you must be patient to buy or sell them at a reasonable price.

Order Types

Preferred stocks may be bought or sold using various types of orders, but caution is required due to their liquidity. Limit orders can be useful to purchase these stocks at reasonable prices, but market and stop loss orders can be a horrible way to buy or sell. The bottom line—handle transactions with care!

Ex-Dividend Date

As with common stock, the ex-dividend date is the date that the stock must be owned to collect an upcoming quarterly dividend. You must own the stock to get the dividend, and be careful not to wait too long to buy the stock (i.e., T-3 settlement rules).

Margin Loan Use

Because many preferreds are marginable (i.e., used as collateral for brokerage house loans), they provide the flexibility to take advantage of investment opportunities. If margin rates are low, then small amounts of margin can be used for a short time to buy new investments at good prices that might not be around when cash is available. In a laddered portfolio, some investments are maturing or being called annually; borrowed funds will be returned when older investments pay back their principal. In other words, this is a cost-effective, medium-risk means to go after long-term investment opportunities.

Short Sell Trading

Since these investments can be illiquid and pay high dividends, short selling (borrowing shares to sell in the hope of making money if an investment drops in value) should be avoided.

Brokerage House Information

Much of the information provided in brokerage house documents (monthly brokerage statements, trade confirmations, and 1099 forms) is confusing. Remember that:

- On most monthly brokerage house statements, a current yield percentage is used that assumes an investor bought the investment at the end of the month. This is generally useless to the investor who has owned the investment prior to the end of the month or owns a floating rate preferred.
- The current values of income investments posted on monthly brokerage statements or daily Web sites are estimated when there is no trading activity for an investment on the date shown. This can cause investors to think that there are "wild" swings in the value of an investment that never really happened!

The old saying "the little things matter" really applies here. The six topics discussed in this section need to be well understood to avoid the mistakes commonly made by investors in preferred stocks.

Chapter 8

Advanced Analysis of the Winans International Preferred Stock Index™ (WIPSI™)

CHART 25–WIPSI Price and Yield
1980 to Present

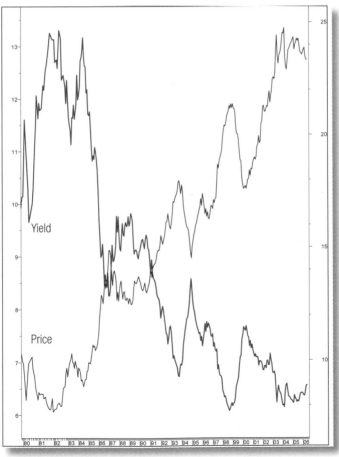

Created in MetaStock from Equis International

Because this is a new index, the purpose of the analysis was limited to determining if common technical approaches would work for identifying changes in the long-term trend (not to provide timing signals for trading). In addition, classic interpretation of charts (i.e., without filters) and default settings on indicators were used. Finally, each indicator was studied individually on its own merits without confirmation from the other indicators.

To make this long-term research easier to follow, the 25-year charts are broken into 5-year charts to support the research segments listed below. Unfortunately, large amounts of volume data were not available.

CHARTS TYPES AND DATA EXAMINED

Weekly data were used to generate bar and candlestick charts for price and yield (CHARTS 26-29). Because the components of the WIPSI™ pay dividends at different times, a total return chart is displayed as a yearly percentage change chart to allow for direct performance comparisons with other investment types (CHART 30). In comparing bar and candlestick charts, it became evident that candlestick charts were more useful, so they were the primary charts used in this analysis.

CHART 26–WIPSI Price Bar Chart
2000-2005

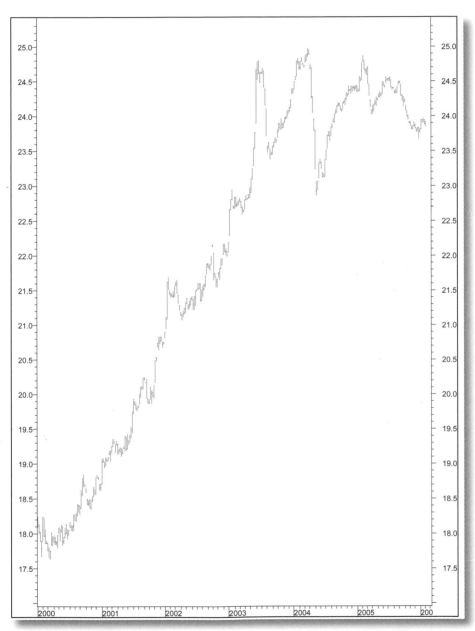

CHART 27—WIPSI™ Yield Bar Chart
2000-2005

CHART 28–WIPSI Price Candlestick Chart
2000-2005

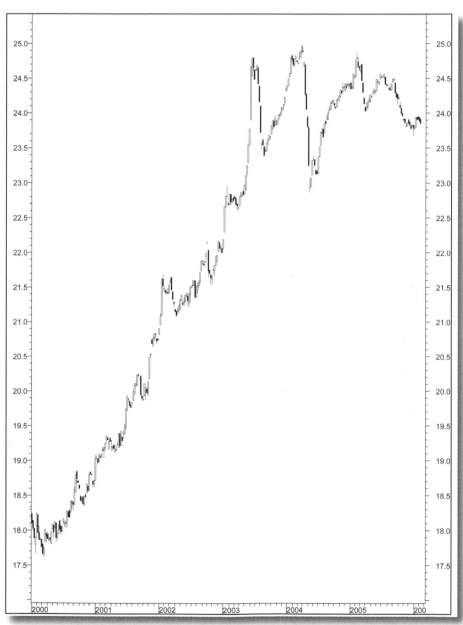

CHART 29–WIPSI™ Yield Candlestick Chart
2000-2005

CHART 30–WIPSI Total Annual Return Chart
1981-2005

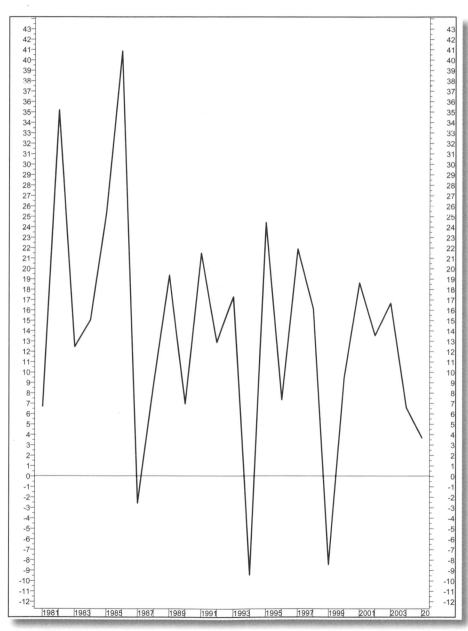

Created in MetaStock from Equis International

CHARTING TECHNIQUES

After inspecting the charts listed in the previous section, the WIPSI™ appeared to meet the requirements needed to conduct effective charting analysis. It displayed the properties of trends, such as long-term advances followed by brief declines within tight ranges. "Data gapping" did not appear to be a problem, as can be the case with many bond indices.

Trendlines

Due to the arbitrary nature of selecting trendlines, inverted yield charts (CHARTS 31-36) were also used to confirm support and resistance points. Also, due to the long time frame covered, both linear (solid) and logarithmic (dotted) trendlines were drawn to help identify long-term support and resistance points.

Signal Rules

- A signal occurred at the first closing price crossing of the trend line.
- Both oversold and overbought signals were observed.
- Trendlines periodically crossed through candle shadows and bodies to have more contact points and best fit the trendline to the data.
- Yield charts must confirm the signal on the price chart.

CHART 31—WIPSI Trendline Analysis, Inverted Yield Chart
1981-2005

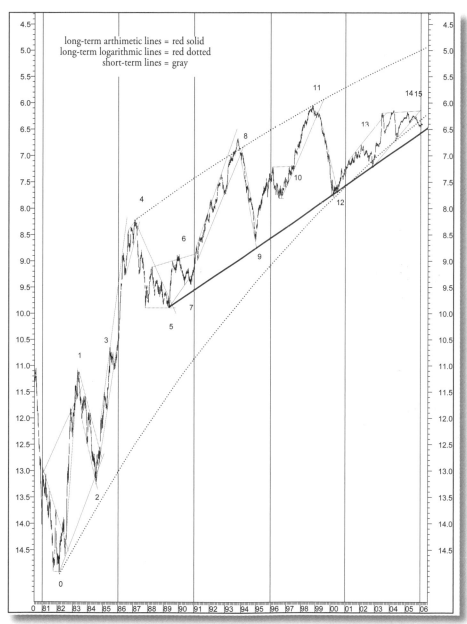

long-term arthimetic lines = red solid
long-term logarithmic lines = red dotted
short-term lines = gray

Created in MetaStock from Equis International

CHART 32–WIPSI Trendline Analysis, Inverted Yield Chart
1981-1985

CHART 33—WIPSI Trendline Analysis, Inverted Yield Chart
1986-1990

CHART 34–WIPSI™ Trendline Analysis, Inverted Yield Chart
1991-1995

Created in MetaStock from Equis International

CHART 35–WIPSI Trendline Analysis, Inverted Yield Chart
1996-2000

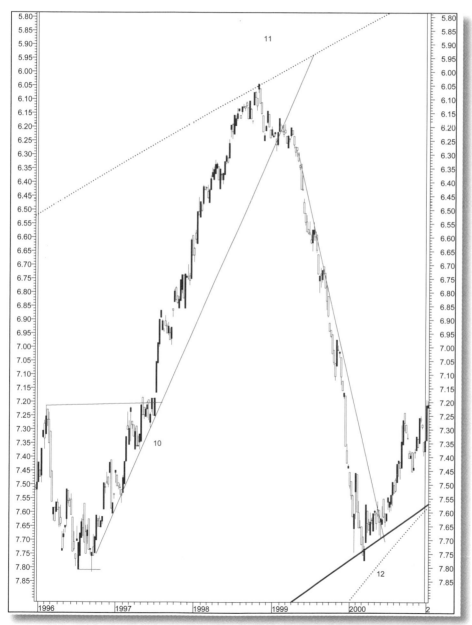

Created in MetaStock from Equis International

CHART 36–WIPSI™ Trendline Analysis, Inverted Yield Chart
2001-2005

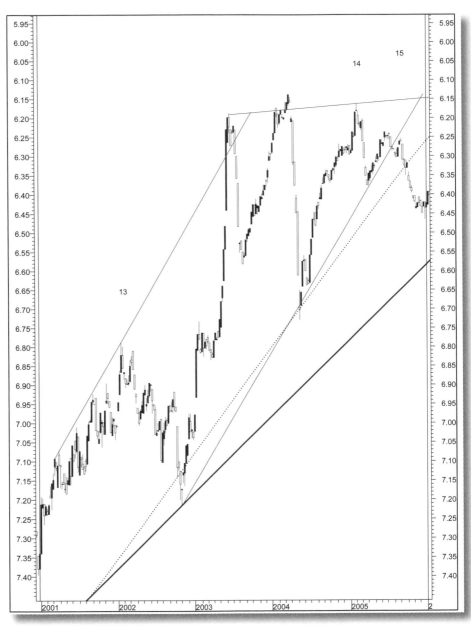

Research Summary (Table 8, Charts 37-42)

There were seven oversold and eight overbought completed signals. The WIPSI had an average advance of 29.2% over 124 weeks from an oversold signal and an average decline of 9.3% over 63 weeks from an overbought signal. With 93% of the signals accurate in indicating the future trend, most of the total move was captured, with the oversold signals happening within 2.1% of the move's low, and overbought signals occurring within -3.2% of the move's high.

TABLE 8–WIPSI™ Trendline Analysis
1981-2005

Signal:	Price:	Signal Date:	Total Move's High:	%	High Date:	Duration Weeks:	From Previous Low:	%	Date	Duration Weeks:	To OB Signal:	%	Date	Duration Weeks:
Oversold (OS):														
0	7.89	02/19/1981	10.60	34.3%	05/06/1983	115	7.88	0.1%	09/25/1981	-31	10.43	32.2%	06/10/1983	120
2	9.04	07/27/1984	15.29	69.1%	02/06/1987	132	9.00	0.4%	07/27/1984	0	14.70	62.6%	04/10/1987	141
5	12.91	05/26/1989	14.17	9.8%	11/24/1989	26	12.66	2.0%	05/19/1989	1	13.87	7.4%	01/26/1990	35
7	13.69	12/21/1990	18.50	35.1%	10/22/1993	148	13.28	3.1%	10/19/1990	9	17.31	26.4%	03/25/1994	170
9	15.36	01/27/1995	17.98	17.1%	02/09/1996	54	14.79	3.9%	12/30/1994	4	17.36	13.0%	03/01/1996	57
10	16.95	07/26/1996	21.80	28.6%	12/01/1998	123	16.49	2.8%	09/13/1996	-7	21.34	25.9%	04/23/1999	143
12	18.09	05/05/2000	24.97	38.0%	03/26/2004	203	17.64	2.6%	03/17/2000	7	24.72	36.7%	04/09/2004	205
Average:				33.2%		114		2.1%		-2		29.2%		124

Signal:	Price:	Signal Date:	Total Move's Low:	%	Low Date:	Duration Weeks:	From Previous High:	%	Date	Duration Weeks:	To OS Signal:	%	Date	Duration Weeks:
Overbought (OB):														
1	10.43	06/10/1983	9.00	-13.7%	07/27/1984	59	10.60	-1.6%	05/06/1983	5	9.04	-13.3%	07/27/1984	59
3	10.97	08/28/1985	10.74	-2.1%	10/04/1985	14	11.25	-2.5%	06/21/1985	1				
4	14.7	04/10/1987	12.83	-12.7%	10/30/1987	29	15.29	-3.9%	02/06/1987	9	12.91	-12.2%	05/26/1989	111
6	13.87	01/26/1990	13.26	-4.4%	05/18/1990	16	14.18	-2.2%	11/24/1989	9	13.69	-1.3%	12/21/1990	47
8	17.31	03/25/1994	14.79	-14.6%	12/30/1994	40	18.50	-6.4%	10/22/1993	22	15.36	-11.3%	01/27/1995	44
9.5	17.36	03/01/1996	16.49	-5.0%	09/13/1996	28	17.98	-3.4%	02/09/1996	3	16.95	-2.4%	07/26/1996	
11	21.34	04/23/1999	17.64	-17.3%	03/17/2000	47	21.80	-2.1%	02/01/1998	64	18.09	-15.2%	05/05/2000	54
13	not confirmed by yield chart													
14	24.72	04/09/2004	22.86	-7.5%	05/24/2004	6	24.97	-1.0%	03/26/2004	2				
15	pending													
Average:				-10.0%		33		-3.2%		16		-9.3%		63

CHART 37–WIPSI Trendline Analysis, Price Chart
1981-2005

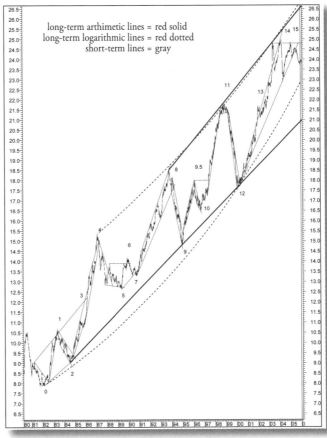

long-term arthimetic lines = red solid
long-term logarithmic lines = red dotted
short-term lines = gray

Created in MetaStock from Equis International

CHART 38–WIPSI Trendline Analysis, Price Chart
1981-1985

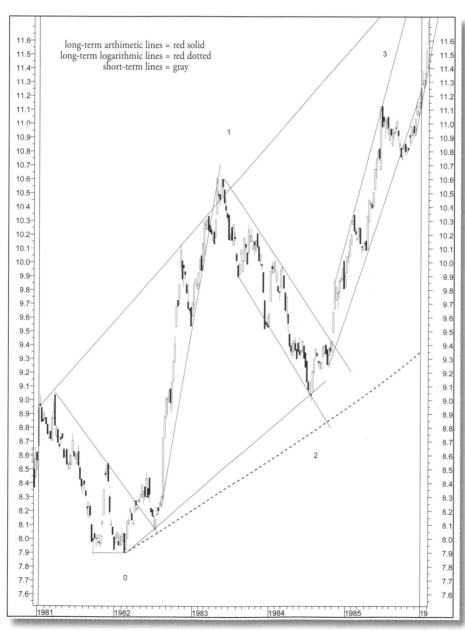

long-term arthimetic lines = red solid
long-term logarithmic lines = red dotted
short-term lines = gray

CHART 39–WIPSI™ Trendline Analysis, Price Chart
1986-1990

long-term arthimetic lines = red solid
long-term logarithmic lines = red dotted
short-term lines = gray

CHART 40–WIPSI Trendline Analysis, Price Chart
1991-1995

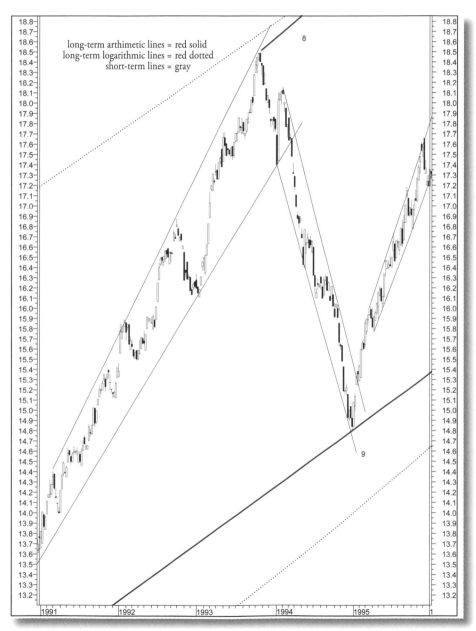

long-term arthimetic lines = red solid
long-term logarithmic lines = red dotted
short-term lines = gray

Created in MetaStock from Equis International

CHART 41—WIPSI™ Trendline Analysis, Price Chart
1996-2000

long-term arthimetic lines = red solid
long-term logarithmic lines = red dotted
short-term lines = gray

Created in MetaStock from Equis International

CHART 42–WIPSI Trendline Analysis, Price Chart
2001-2005

long-term arthimetic lines = red solid
long-term logarithmic lines = red dotted
short-term lines = gray

Created in MetaStock from Equis International

Regression Lines and Standard Error Channels

Chart analysis can be very subjective, so an automated way to draw trendlines was used for identifying them. Least squares linear regression analysis is a statistical tool that plots a line through prices, which helps minimize the distance between the prices and the resulting trendlines. Standard error analysis can help determine where the "extremes" lie—and predict trends and changes in trends before they happen.

Signal Rules

- A signal occurred at the first crossing of the standard error channel by the full body of a candlestick.
- Channels had to be at least one year in length.
- Repeat signals were ignored.
- The high or low of the previous move was used as the start point of the next channel.
- Both oversold and overbought signals were observed.

Research Summary (TABLE 9, CHARTS 43-48)

There were six oversold and five overbought completed signals. The index had an average advance of 24.4% over 129 weeks from an oversold signal and an average decline of 4.4% over 74 weeks from an overbought signal. Although 91% of the signals were accurate in indicating the future trend, the overbought signals gave up too much "ground." For example, the oversold signals were only 6.8% from the low of the move, but the overbought signals gave up -5.8% from the move's high (which was more than 50% of the entire move).

TABLE 9–WIPSI™ Regression and Standard Error Analysis
1981-2005

WIPSI Regression/Standard Error Analysis:

Signal:	Number:	Price:	Signal Date:	Total Move's High:	%	High Date:	Duration Weeks:	From Previous Low:	%	Date	Duration Weeks:	To OB Signal:	%	Date	Duration Weeks:
Oversold (OS)	1	8.38	05/14/1982	10.60	26.5%	05/06/1983	51	7.90	6.1%	02/12/1982	13	10.17	21.4%	07/29/1983	63
	3	9.64	11/09/1984	15.30	58.7%	02/06/1987	117	9.00	7.1%	07/27/1984	15	13.80	43.2%	05/15/1987	131
	5	13.65	07/07/1989	18.50	35.5%	10/15/1993	223	12.66	7.8%	05/19/1989	7	16.99	24.5%	04/08/1994	248
	7	15.91	04/14/1995	17.98	13.0%	02/09/1996	43	14.79	7.6%	12/30/1994	15	16.95	6.5%	04/19/1996	53
	9	18.09	06/13/1997	21.80	20.5%	12/04/1998	77	16.49	9.7%	09/13/1996	39	21.53	19.0%	12/25/1998	80
	11	18.05	06/30/2000	24.97	38.3%	03/26/2004	195	17.64	2.3%	03/17/2000	15	23.79	31.8%	04/30/2004	200
Average:					32.1%		118		6.8%		17		24.4%		129
Median:					31.0%		97		7.3%		15		22.9%		106

Overbought (OB):	Number:	Price:	Signal Date:	Total Move's Low:	%	Low Date:	Duration Weeks:	High:	%	Date	Duration Weeks:	To OS Signal:	%	Date	Duration Weeks:
	2	10.17	07/29/1983	9.00	-11.5%	07/27/1984	52	10.60	-4.1%	05/06/1983	12	9.64	6.2%	11/09/1984	67
	4	13.8	05/15/1987	12.66	-8.3%	05/19/1989	105	15.30	-9.8%	02/06/1987	14	13.65	-1.1%	07/07/1989	112
	6	16.99	04/08/1994	14.79	-12.9%	12/30/1994	38	18.50	-8.2%	10/15/1993	25	15.91	-6.4%	04/14/1995	53
	8	16.95	04/19/1996	16.49	-2.7%	09/13/1996	21	17.98	-5.7%	02/09/1996	10	18.09	6.7%	06/13/1997	60
	10	21.53	12/25/1998	17.64	-18.1%	03/17/2000	64	21.80	-1.2%	12/04/1998	3	18.05	-16.2%	06/30/2000	79
	12	23.79	04/30/2004												
Average:					-10.7%		56		-5.8%		13		-4.4%		74
Median:					-11.5%		52		-5.7%		12		-5.2%		67

CHART 43–WIPSI Regression Analysis
1981-2005

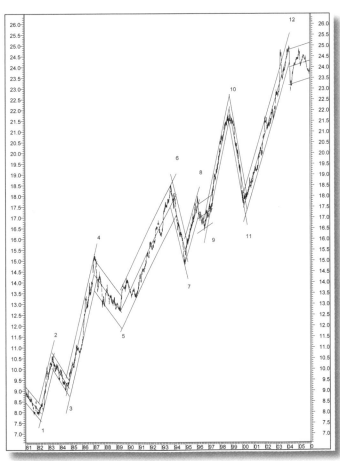

Created in MetaStock from Equis International

Chart 44–WIPSI™ Regression Analysis
1981-1985

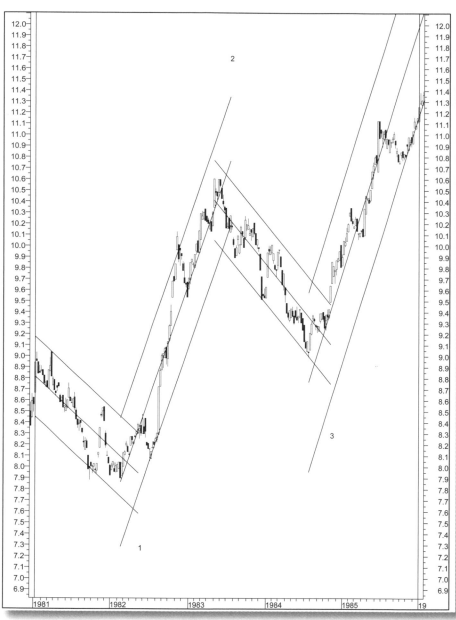

CHART 45–WIPSI Regression Analysis
1986-1990

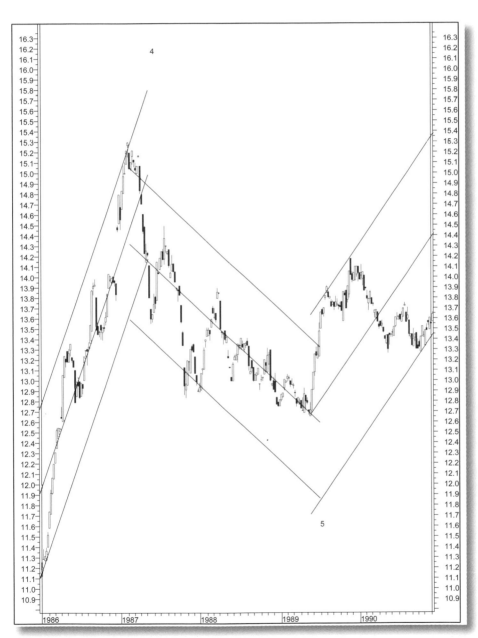

Created in MetaStock from Equis International

CHART 46–WIPSI™ Regression Analysis
1991-1995

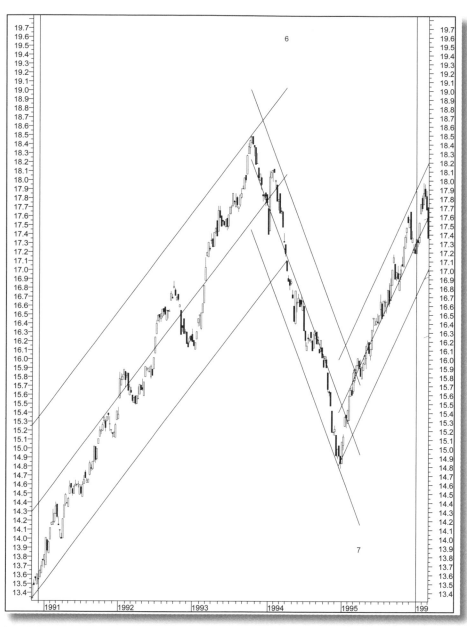

CHART 47–WIPSI Regression Analysis
1996-2000

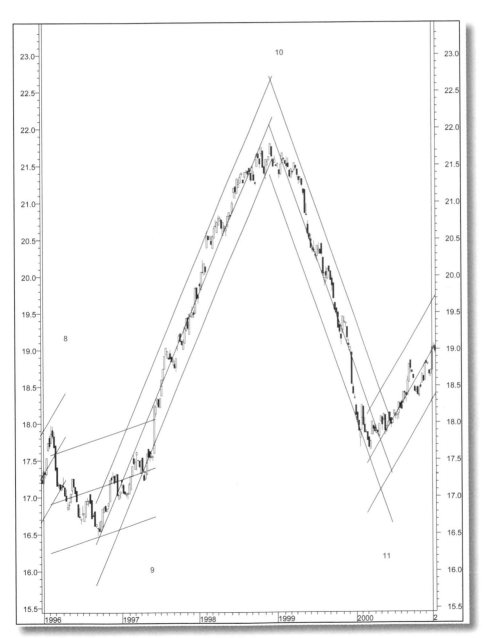

CHART 48–WIPSI™ Regression Analysis
2001-2005

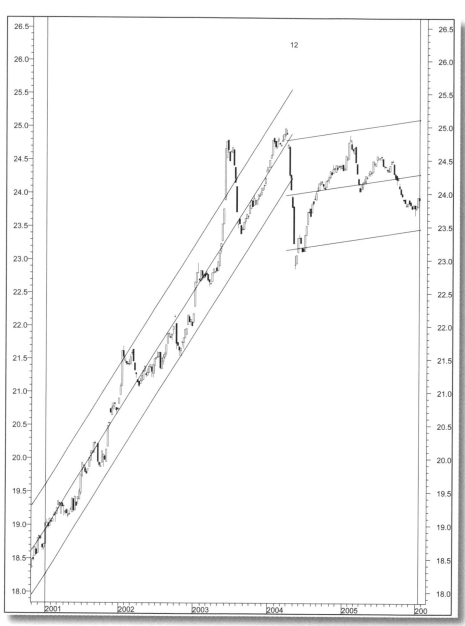

MOVING AVERAGES

In analyzing the simple, weighted, and exponential moving averages for 10, 20, and 40 weeks, the first objective was to identify the moving averages that had the fewest false signals. As can be seen on CHARTS 49 and 50, the 10- and 20-week moving averages would require a filter such as the 2-week or 3% penetration rule to be a useful long-term indicator. In reviewing the 40-week moving averages on CHART 51, the simple moving average had 46% fewer false signals than either the weighted or exponential moving averages and thus was the focus of this study.

Signal Rules
- A crossing of the closing price above or below the simple moving average.
- Both oversold and overbought signals were observed.

CHART 49–WIPSI™ Moving Average Analysis (10-Week)
2000-2005

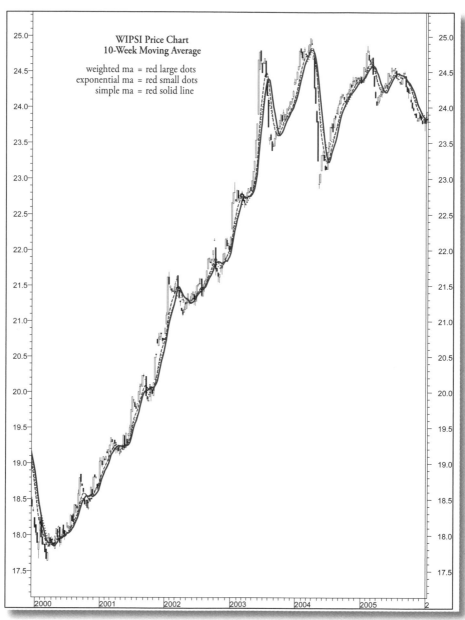

WIPSI Price Chart
10-Week Moving Average

weighted ma = red large dots
exponential ma = red small dots
simple ma = red solid line

CHART 50–WIPSI Moving Average Analysis (20-Week)
2000-2005

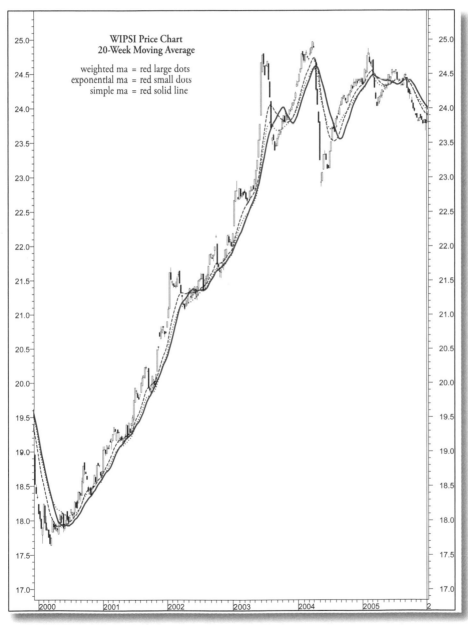

WIPSI Price Chart
20-Week Moving Average

weighted ma = red large dots
exponential ma = red small dots
simple ma = red solid line

Created in MetaStock from Equis International

CHART 51–WIPSI™ Moving Average Analysis (40-Week, Incorrect Crossings)
1981-2005

WIPSI Price Chart
40-Week Moving Average Incorrect Crossings

weighted ma = red large dots 9 signals
exponential ma = red small dots 9 signals
simple ma = red solid line 5 signals
All ma Signaled = 7 signals

Research Summary (Table 10, Charts 52-57)

There were eight oversold and seven overbought completed signals. The index had an average advance of 21.1% over 100 weeks from an oversold signal and an average decline of 5.3% over 58 weeks from an overbought signal. Although 87% of the signals were accurate in indicating the future trend, the overbought signals gave up too much "ground" when compared to other technical tools. For example, the oversold signals were only 4.5% from the low of the move, and the overbought signals gave up -4.3% off the high of the move (which was 45% of the entire change).

TABLE 10–WIPSI™ 40-Week Moving Average Analysis
1981-2005

Signal:	Number:	Price:	Signal Date	Total Move's High:	%	High Date:	Duration Weeks:	From Previous Low:	%	Date	Duration Weeks:	To OB Signal:	%	Date	Duration Weeks:
Oversold (OS):	1	8.21	03/19/1982	10.60	29.1%	05/06/1983	59	7.90	3.9%	02/19/1982	4	10.01	21.9%	08/05/1983	72
	3	9.64	11/09/1984	15.30	58.7%	02/06/1987	117	9.00	7.1%	07/27/1984	15	14.23	47.6%	04/24/1987	128
	5	13.08	06/02/1989	14.18	8.4%	11/24/1989	25	12.66	3.3%	05/19/1989	2	13.75	5.1%	03/02/1990	39
	7	13.55	11/23/1990	18.49	36.5%	10/23/1993	152	13.27	2.1%	10/19/1990	5	17.75	31.0%	12/31/1993	162
	9	15.89	03/10/1995	17.86	12.4%	02/09/1996	48	14.76	7.7%	12/30/1994	10	17.02	7.1%	04/12/1996	57
	11	17.23	11/08/1996	21.80	26.5%	12/04/1998	108	16.48	4.6%	09/13/1996	8	21.35	23.9%	03/05/1999	121
	13	18.19	08/04/2000	24.97	37.3%	03/26/2004	190	17.75	2.5%	03/17/2000	20	24.05	32.2%	04/23/2004	194
	15	24.11	10/01/2004	24.87	3.2%	02/11/2005	19	22.93	5.1%	05/14/2004	20	24.14	0.1%	03/25/2005	25
Average:					26.5%		90		4.5%		11		21.1%		100
Median:					27.8%		84		4.2%		9		22.9%		97
				Low:				High:				To OS Signal:			
Overbought (OB):	2	10.01	08/05/1983	9.00	-10.1%	07/27/1984	51	10.60	-5.6%	05/06/1983	13	9.64	-3.7%	11/09/1984	66
	4	14.23	04/24/1987	12.66	-11.0%	05/19/1989	108	15.30	-7.0%	02/06/1987	11	13.08	-8.1%	06/02/1989	110
	6	13.75	03/02/1990	13.27	-3.5%	10/19/1990	33	14.18	-3.0%	11/24/1989	14	13.55	-1.5%	11/23/1990	38
	8	17.75	12/31/1993	14.76	-16.8%	12/30/1994	52	18.49	-4.0%	10/23/1993	10	15.89	-10.5%	03/10/1995	62
	10	17.02	04/12/1996	16.48	-3.2%	09/13/1996	22	17.86	-4.7%	02/09/1996	9	17.23	1.2%	11/08/1996	30
	12	21.35	03/05/1999	17.75	-16.9%	03/17/2000	54	21.80	-2.1%	12/04/1998	13	18.19	-14.8%	08/04/2000	74
	14	24.05	04/23/2004	22.93	-4.7%	05/14/2004	3	24.97	-3.7%	03/26/2004	4	24.11	0.2%	10/01/2004	23
Average:				-9.5%		46		-4.3%		11		-5.3%		58
Median:				-10.1%		51		-4.0%		11		-3.7%		62

CHART 52–WIPSI Moving Average Analysis (40-Week)
1981-2005

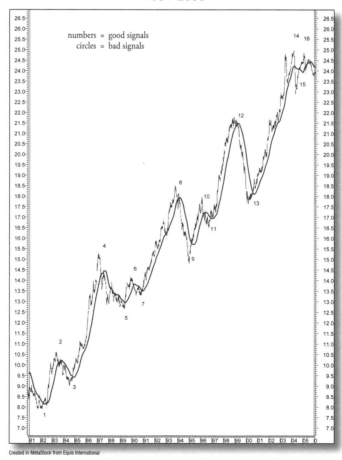

numbers = good signals
circles = bad signals

Created in MetaStock from Equis International

CHART 53–WIPSI Moving Average Analysis (40-Week)
1981-1985

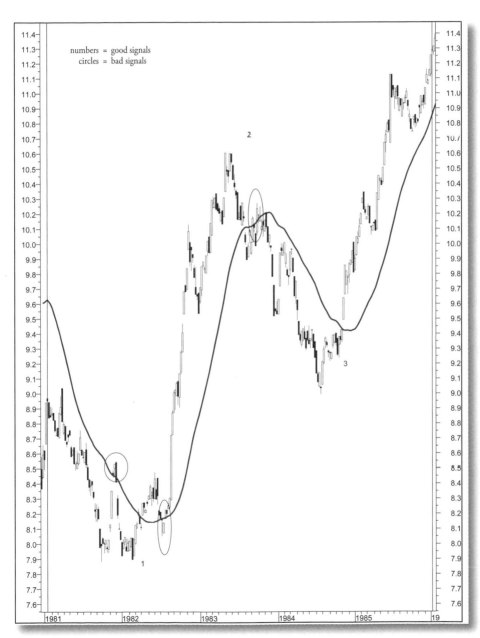

numbers = good signals
circles = bad signals

CHART 54—WIPSI™ Moving Average Analysis (40-Week)
1986-1990

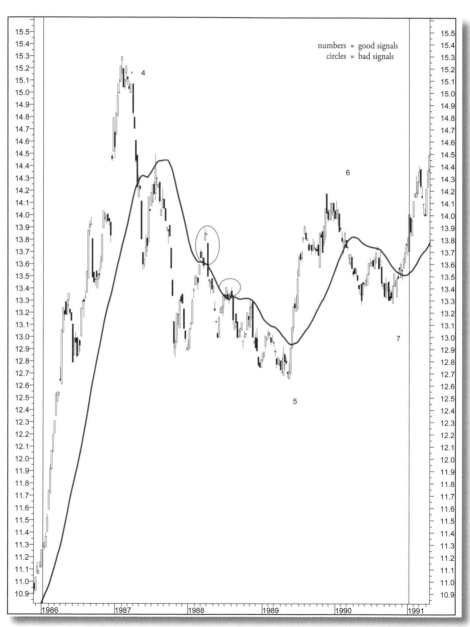

numbers = good signals
circles = bad signals

Created in MetaStock from Equis International

CHART 55–WIPSI Moving Average Analysis (40-Week)
1991-1995

CHART 56–WIPSI™ Moving Average Analysis (40-Week)
1996-2000

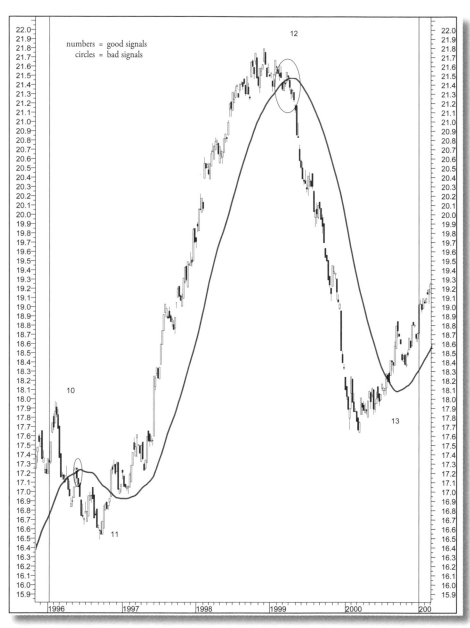

numbers = good signals
circles = bad signals

CHART 57–WIPSI Moving Average Analysis (40-Week)
2001-2005

numbers = good signals
circles = bad signals

OSCILLATORS

The Wilder Relative Strength (RSI) and Stochastic Indicators were picked because of their popularity with investors. Although oscillators are primarily used in "sideways" markets (i.e., trading ranges), the primary focus was on whether these indicators would prove useful for providing oversold signals in a long-term uptrend.

RSI Signal Rules

- The 14 periods calculation was used.
- The focus was placed on 70 and 30 crossover points.
- The first signal was used with secondary signals only for confirmation.
- Only oversold signals were observed.

Research Summary (Table 11, Chart 58)

Seven oversold signals were followed by an average advance of 31.4% over 140 weeks. With 86% of the signals accurate in indicating the future trend, the oversold signals were only 3.5% from the low of the move. If median calculations are used to reduce the effect of the one false signal, then the average signal was only 2.1% from the low. Although not consistent enough to be used as an overbought signal, seven overbought failure swings were identified, with four occurring at or near significant tops.

TABLE 11—WIPSI™ RSI (Wilder) Analysis
1981-2005

Signal:	Number:	price:	Signal date:	Total Move's High:	%	High date:	duration weeks:	From Previous Low:	%	date	duration weeks:
Oversold (OS)	1	8.03	10/31/1981	10.60	32.0%	05/06/1983	79	7.90	1.6%	09/25/1981	5
	2	9.14	07/20/1984	15.30	67.4%	02/06/1987	133	9.04	1.1%	07/20/1984	0
	3	13.19	11/06/1987	14.18	7.5%	11/24/1989	107	12.83	2.8%	10/30/1987	1
	4	13.43	05/25/1990	18.51	37.8%	10/15/1993	177	13.26	1.3%	05/18/1990	1
	5	16.77	05/20/1994	21.80	30.0%	12/04/1998	237	14.78	13.5%	12/30/1994	-32
	6	18.01	03/24/2000	24.97	38.6%	03/26/2004	209	17.64	2.1%	03/17/2000	1
	7	23.33	05/28/2004	24.87	6.6%	02/11/2005	37	22.86	2.1%	05/14/2004	2
Average:					31.4%		140		3.6%		-3
Median:					32.0%		133		2.1%		1

CHART 58—WIPSI RSI Analysis
1981-2005

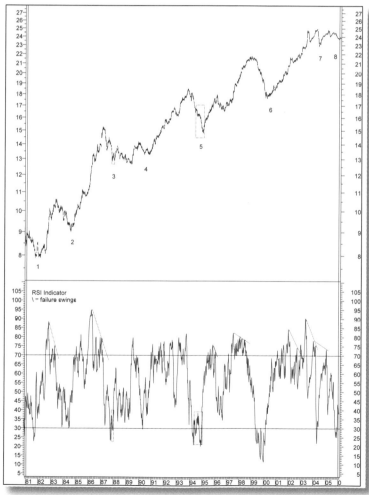

Created in MetaStock from Equis International

Slow Stochastic Signal Rules
- The 14 period k% calculation with the 3 period average of d% was used.
- The focus was placed on 80 and 20 values with a crossing of the %k line below and above the %d line.
- Only oversold signals were observed.

Research Summary (Chart 59)

The Stochastic Indicator was much more sensitive than the RSI indicator with approximately 81 individual signals. With such a large number of signals and no filtering, the number of false signals made this an unreliable long-term indicator for the WIPSI™.

CHART 59–WIPSI Stochastic Analysis
1981-2005

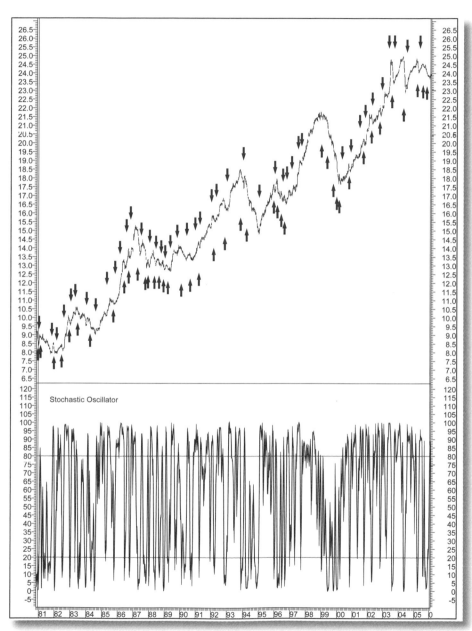

RELATIVE STRENGTH (RATIO CHARTS)

To make direct comparisons of the WIPSI™ with corporate bonds, ratio charts were developed for price (WIPSI/Dow Jones Corporate Bond 20 Index) and yield (WIPSI Yield/Moody's BAA Corporate Bond Yield).

WIPSI/Dow Jones Corporate Bond Index Ratio

Although their individual charts look very similar (CHARTS 60-61), the ratio chart clearly shows weakness in the WIPSI versus the bond index (CHART 62) by the violation of the trend line drawn.

CHART 60–WIPSI Price Chart
1981-2005

Created in MetaStock from Equis International

CHART 61–Dow Jones
Corporate Bond 20 Index
Price Chart
1981-2005

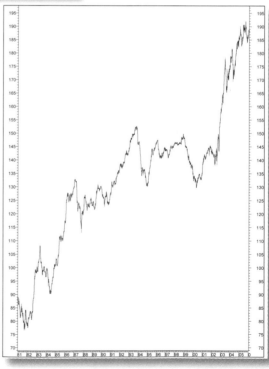

CHART 62–WIPSI™/ Dow Jones Corporate Bond 20 Index Ratio Chart
1981-2005

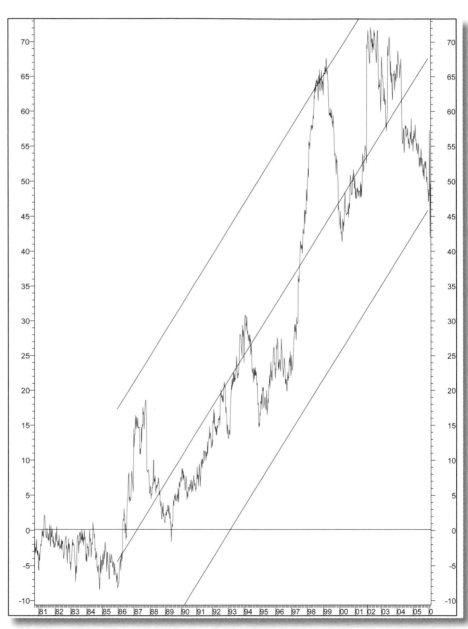

WIPSI Yield/Moody's Rated BAA Corporate Bonds Yield Ratio (CHART 63)

When you compare the yields of these two investment types, it shows that yields of the WIPSI are rarely less than 81 basis points of BAA bonds. Also depicted: The current preferred yield is near a 25-year high in relation to bond yields with a similar rating to the WIPSI.

CHART 63–WIPSI Yield/Moody's BAA Yield Ratio Chart
1981-2005

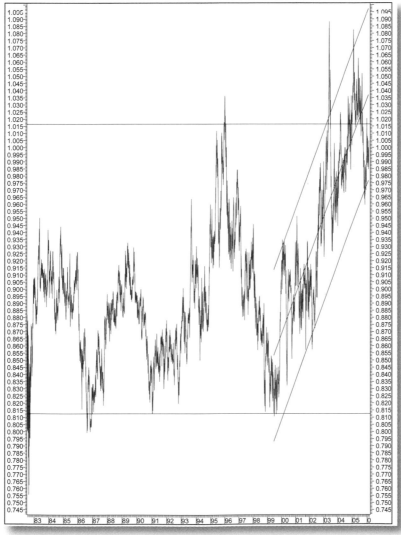

Created in MetaStock from Equis International

Total Return Charts (TABLE 12, CHARTS 64, 65)

In comparing the total return of the WIPSI™ and the Dow Jones Corporate Bond 20 Index, a very similar pattern exists between yearly returns.

TABLE 12—WIPSI and Dow Jones Corporate Bond 20 Index Annual Returns
1981-2005

		WIPSI					Dow Jones		
Year-end	Index Value	Yr to Yr % Change	Beginning of Year Yield	Total Return	Year-end	Index Value	Yr to Yr % Change	Beginning of Year Yield	Total Return
1980	8.58				1980	88.59			
1981	7.99	-6.9%	13.61%	6.73%	1981	79.41	-10.4%	12.9%	2.5%
1982	9.62	20.4%	14.79%	35.19%	1982	98.29	23.8%	14.8%	38.6%
1983	9.63	0.1%	12.36%	12.46%	1983	97.03	-1.3%	12.1%	10.8%
1984	9.88	2.6%	12.46%	15.06%	1984	100.79	3.9%	12.4%	16.3%
1985	11.19	13.3%	12.18%	25.44%	1985	116.47	15.6%	12.3%	27.9%
1986	14.57	30.2%	10.65%	40.86%	1986	129.98	11.6%	10.5%	22.1%
1987	12.93	-11.3%	8.69%	-2.57%	1987	120.82	-7.0%	9.3%	2.3%
1988	12.81	-0.9%	9.77%	8.84%	1988	123.24	2.0%	10.3%	12.3%
1989	14.04	9.6%	9.76%	19.36%	1989	129.29	4.9%	10.0%	14.9%
1990	13.76	-2.0%	8.96%	6.97%	1990	127.39	-1.5%	9.3%	7.8%
1991	15.46	12.4%	9.12%	21.47%	1991	137.35	7.8%	9.5%	17.3%
1992	16.2	4.8%	8.09%	12.88%	1992	143.72	4.6%	8.5%	13.1%
1993	17.75	9.6%	7.69%	17.26%	1993	145.86	1.5%	7.3%	8.8%
1994	14.84	-16.4%	6.97%	-9.42%	1994	130.16	-10.8%	6.2%	-4.6%
1995	17.19	15.8%	8.58%	24.42%	1995	146.53	12.6%	8.2%	20.8%
1996	17.17	-0.1%	7.49%	7.37%	1996	144.37	-1.5%	6.9%	5.4%
1997	19.64	14.4%	7.50%	21.89%	1997	146.14	1.2%	7.2%	8.4%
1998	21.49	9.4%	6.69%	16.11%	1998	147.96	1.2%	6.9%	8.1%
1999	18.34	-14.7%	6.23%	-8.43%	1999	135.82	-8.2%	6.5%	-1.7%
2000	18.71	2.0%	7.43%	9.45%	2000	135.44	-0.3%	7.8%	7.5%
2001	20.82	11.3%	7.34%	18.62%	2001	143.69	6.1%	8.1%	14.2%
2002	22.19	6.6%	6.97%	13.55%	2002	159.23	10.8%	7.3%	18.1%
2003	24.34	9.7%	6.98%	16.67%	2003	174.68	9.7%	5.5%	15.2%
2004	24.41	0.3%	6.29%	6.58%	2004	185.23	6.0%	4.7%	10.7%
2005	23.78	-2.6%	6.28%	3.70%	2005	188.48	1.8%	4.9%	6.7%
Average		4.7%	8.7%	**14%**	Average		3.4%	8.8%	**12%**
Cumulative Change		184.5%	222.9%	**407%**	Cumulative Change		42.5%	219.4%	**262%**

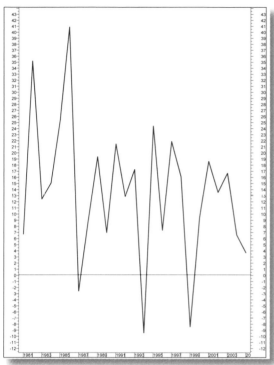

Created in MetaStock from Equis International

Cʜᴀʀᴛ 64–WIPSI
Total Annual Return Chart
1981-2005

Cʜᴀʀᴛ 65–Dow Jones
Corporate Bond 20 Index
Total Annual Return Chart
1981-2005

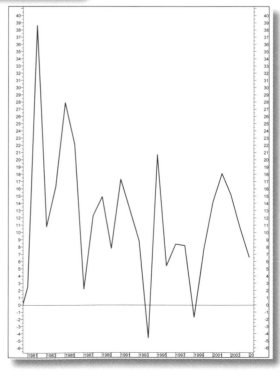

Chapter 9

Advanced Analysis of Individual Preferred Stocks

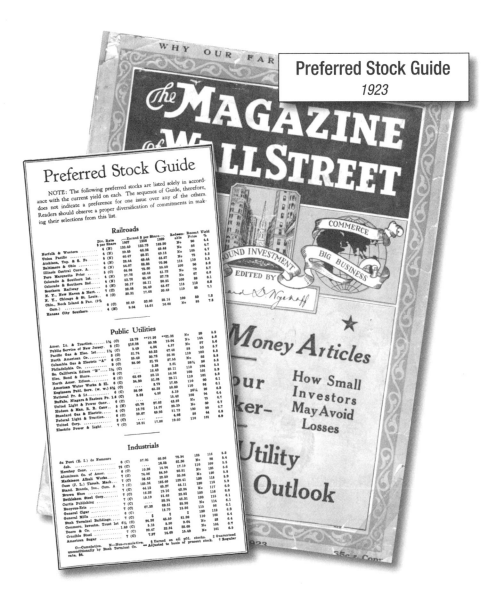

Preferred Stock Guide
1923

The purpose of this analysis was to determine if common technical approaches can identify long-term changes in the trends of preferred stocks. As in the case of the WIPSI™, this is "virgin territory" that had not been analyzed, so classic interpretations of charts (i.e., without filters) and default settings on indicators were used. An eight-year scope (1998-2005) was selected, using weekly data for price and volume (bar charts at the bottom of each chart), because most individual preferred stocks have a limited life. Yield charts were not used.

INDIVIDUAL PREFERRED STOCKS USED IN THIS ANALYSIS

Selection Process—three straight, nonconvertible preferred stocks were selected for the following reasons.

- These stocks display the trading characteristics of most preferred stocks that actively trade. To make comparisons to the WIPSI meaningful, the focus of the research was on straight preferred stocks.
- They are from industries that have historically issued preferred stocks (i.e., Alcoa–manufacturing, Consolidated Edison–utility, Merrill Lynch–finance) and are components of the WIPSI.
- They have continuously traded since 1998. Most preferred stocks have actively traded for less than five years, and price data on called or retired preferred stocks were not available.

DATA FILTERING

In addition to the selection criteria, the price and volume data had to be carefully screened for inaccuracies caused by periodic illiquidity. Note: Price gaps caused by quarterly dividends being paid were considered in the selection process.

Each indicator was examined individually on its own merits without confirmation from other indicators. Every research segment listed below is supported by eight-year charts.

CHARTS AND DATA EXAMINED

The individual preferred stocks selected (Alcoa Series A [AA], Consolidated Edison Series A [ED] and Merrill Lynch Series B [MER]) have had high, low. and volume figures daily for eight years. To make direct comparisons to the WIPSI and avoid problems with a day in which a stock did not trade, weekly data were used to generate charts for price and volume. As with the WIPSI, candlestick charts were more useful and were the primary chart used in this report.

CHARTING TECHNIQUES AND VOLUME INTERPRETATION

Upon initial inspection of the charts listed above, the preferred stocks appeared to have the elements needed to conduct effective analysis. Volume was used to help confirm price movements. Special attention was placed at resistance, support, and reversal points, where volume was expected to decline at bottoms, as selling pressure subsides, and at resistance points that could not be penetrated. Furthermore, volume was expected to increase at breakouts and breakdowns.

Trendlines

Due to the arbitrary nature of selecting trendlines, reasonable judgment was given to selecting areas that would be easy to identify.

Signal Rules

- A signal occurred at the first closing price crossing of the trendline.
- Both oversold and overbought signals were observed.
- Trendlines periodically crossed through candlestick shadows and bodies to have more contact points and best fit the trendline to the data.
- Volume was used to confirm the price signal.

Research Summary (Table 13, Charts 66-68)

The stocks posted 10 oversold and 10 overbought completed signals. They had an average advance of 18% over 80 weeks from an oversold signal and an average decline of 8.4% over 22 weeks from an overbought signal. With 75% of the signals accurate in indicating the future trend, most of the move was captured with the oversold signals occurring within 7.5% of the move's low. However, the overbought signals gave up too much "ground." For example, the overbought signals gave up -7.3% from the move's high (which was more than 50% of the entire move).

TABLE 13–Preferred Stock Trendline Analysis
1998-2005

Preferred Stock Trendlines Analysis:

Signal	Price	Signal Date	Total Move's High:	%	High Date:	From Previous Low:	%	Date	Duration Weeks:	To OB Signal:	%	Date	Duration Weeks:
Oversold (OS):													
AA2	54.5	07/18/2000	88.00	61.5%	07/02/2003	50.63	7.6%	07/11/2000	1	88.00	61.5%	07/02/2003	154
AA4	78.5	09/12/2003	85.90	9.4%	03/04/2004	72.75	7.9%	09/12/2003	0	75.00	-4.5%	04/30/2004	33
AA6	73	06/18/2004	84.00	15.1%	02/04/2005	71.50	2.1%	06/18/2004	0	79.50	8.9%	03/02/2005	37
AA8	Pending												
ED2	63.75	05/12/2000	99.00	55.3%	06/13/2003	59.50	7.1%	03/30/2000	6	95.01	49.0%	07/03/2003	164
ED3	72.55	08/10/2001	99.00	36.5%	06/13/2003	59.50	21.9%	03/30/2000	71	95.01	31.0%	07/03/2003	99
ED6	92.35	11/21/2003	97.05	5.1%	04/08/2004	85.03	8.6%	08/08/2003	15	91.00	-1.5%	04/23/2004	22
ED8	83.42	05/21/2004	93.25	11.8%	07/15/2005	79.00	5.6%	05/14/2004	1	93.25	11.8%	07/15/2005	60
MER2	22.88	05/26/2002	28.78	25.8%	06/20/2003	20.88	9.6%	12/31/1999	21	27.25	19.1%	04/25/2003	152
MER3	Not Confirmed by Volume												
MER3.5	27.25	04/25/2003	28.78	5.6%	06/20/2003	26.50	2.8%	04/25/2003	0	27.14	-0.4%	04/08/2004	50
MER5	25.8	05/14/2004	27.54	6.7%	09/24/2004	25.50	1.2%	05/14/2004	0	27.15	5.2%	12/23/2004	32
Average:				23.3%			**7.5%**		12		**18.0%**		**80**
Median:				13.4%			7.4%		1		10.3%		55
Overbought (OB):			Low:			High:				To OS Signal			
AA1	68	07/29/1999	50.63	-25.5%	07/11/2000	78.00	-12.8%	01/08/1999	29	54.50	-19.9%	07/18/2000	51
AA3	88	07/02/2003	75.00	-14.8%	04/30/2004	88.00	0.0%	07/02/2003	0	78.50	-10.8%	09/12/2003	10
AA5	75	04/30/2004	74.25	-1.0%	03/24/2005	88.00	-14.8%	07/02/2003	43	73.00	-2.7%	06/18/2004	7
AA7	79.5	03/02/2005	74.25	-6.6%	03/24/2005	84.00	-5.4%	02/04/2005	4	74.25	-6.6%	03/24/2005	3
ED1	84.25	04/16/1999	59.50	-29.4%	03/30/2000	92.00	-8.4%	10/30/1998	24	63.75	-24.3%	05/12/2000	56
ED4	95.01	07/03/2003	85.03	-10.5%	08/08/2003	99.00	-4.0%	06/13/2003	3	92.35	-2.8%	11/21/2003	20
ED5	85.8	08/08/2003	85.03	-0.9%	08/08/2003	99.00	-13.3%	03/30/2000	175	92.35	7.6%	11/21/2003	15
ED7	91	04/23/2004	79.00	-13.2%	05/14/2004	97.05	-6.2%	04/23/2004	0	83.42	-8.3%	05/21/2004	4
ED9	Pending												
MER1	25.88	06/18/1999	20.88	-19.3%	12/31/1999	26.50	-2.3%	12/24/1998	25	22.88	-11.6%	05/26/2000	49
MER4	27.14	04/08/2004	25.25	-7.0%	05/14/2004	28.78	-5.7%	06/20/2003	42	25.80	-4.9%	05/14/2004	5
MER6	Pending												
Average:				-12.8%			**-7.3%**		34		**-8.4%**		**22**
Median:				-11.8%			-6.0%		25		-7.5%		13

CHART 66–Preferred Stock Trendline Analysis, Alcoa pf A
1998-2005

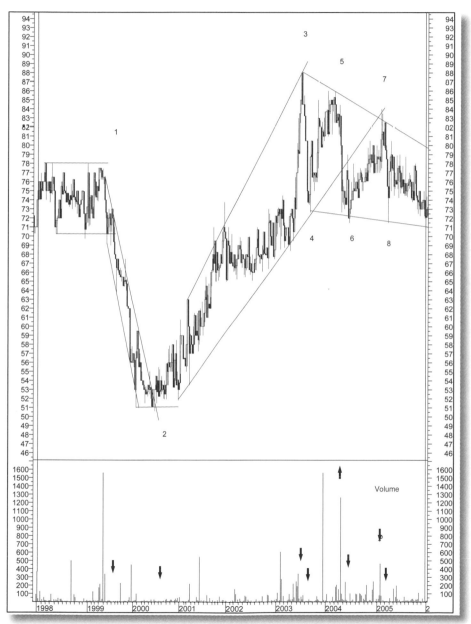

Created in MetaStock from Equis International

Chart 67–Preferred Stock Trendline Analysis, Consolidated Edison pf A
1998-2005

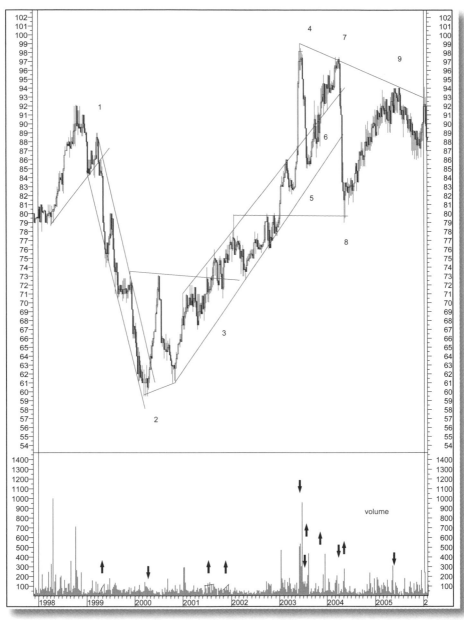

Created in MetaStock from Equis International

CHART 68—Preferred Stock Trendline Analysis, Merrill Lynch pf B
1998-2005

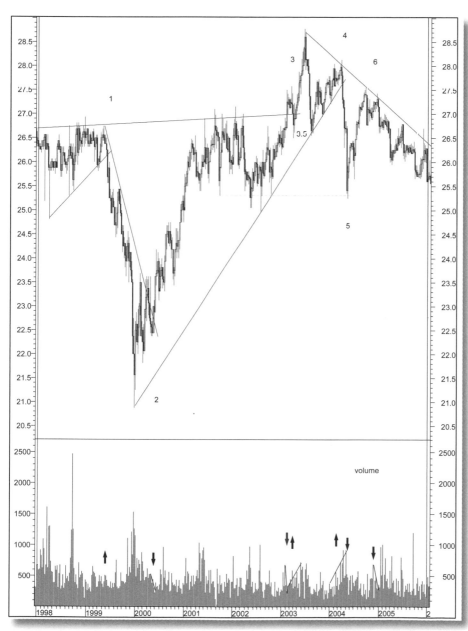

Regression Lines and Standard Error Channels

Because chart analysis can be very subjective, an automated way to draw trendlines was needed for identifying trends. Least squares linear regression analysis is a statistical tool that plots a line through prices; it's designed to minimize the distance between the prices and the resulting trendlines. Standard error analysis helps determine where statistical "extremes" lie, which is useful in identifying trends and changes in them.

Signal Rules

- A signal occurred at the first crossing of the standard error channel by the body of a candlestick.
- Channels had to be at least one year in length.
- Repeat signals were ignored.
- The high or low of the previous move was used as the start point of the next channel.
- Both oversold and overbought signals were observed.

Research Summary (Table 14, Charts 69-71)

There were four oversold and four overbought completed signals. The stocks had an average advance of 32% over 124 weeks from an oversold signal and an average decline of 12.9% during 42 weeks by an overbought signal. Seventy-five percent of the signals were accurate in indicating the future trend. However, the signals gave up a lot of "ground." For example, the oversold signals were 9.8% from the low of the move, while the overbought signals gave up -5.1% from the change's high.

TABLE 14–Preferred Stock Regression Analysis
1998-2005

Preferred Stocks Regression/Standard Error Analysis:

Signal:	Price:	Signal Date:	Total Move's High:	%	High Date:	From Previous Low:	%	Date	Duration Weeks:	To OB Signal:	%	Date	Duration Weeks:
Oversold													
AA1	54.5	07/18/2000	88.00	61.5%	07/02/2003	50.63	7.6%	07/11/2000	1	88.00	61.5%	07/02/2003	154
ED5	63.75	05/12/2000	99.00	55.3%	06/13/2003	59.50	7.1%	03/30/2000	6	95.01	49.0%	07/03/2003	164
ED11	72.55	08/10/2001	99.00	36.5%	06/13/2003	59.50	21.9%	03/30/2000	71	95.01	31.0%	07/03/2003	99
MER4	22.88	05/26/2000	28.78	25.8%	06/20/2003	20.88	9.6%	12/31/1999	21	27.25	19.1%	04/25/2003	152
MER7	27.25	04/25/2003	28.78	5.6%	06/20/2003	26.50	2.8%	04/25/2003	0	27.14	-0.4%	04/08/2004	50
Average:				36.9%			9.8%		20		32.0%		124
Median:				36.5%			7.6%		6		31.0%		152
Overbought:			Low:			High:				To OS Signal			
AA3	Pending												
ED2	84.25	04/16/1999	59.50	-29.4%	03/30/2000	92.00	-8.4%	10/30/1998	24	63.75	-24.3%	05/12/2000	56
ED10	95.01	07/03/2003	85.03	-10.5%	08/08/2003	99.00	-4.0%	06/13/2003	3	92.35	-2.8%	11/21/2003	20
MER5	25.88	06/18/1999	20.88	-19.3%	12/31/1999	26.50	-2.3%	12/24/1998	25	22.88	-11.6%	05/26/2000	49
MER6	27.14	04/08/2004	25.25	-7.0%	05/14/2004	28.78	-5.7%	06/20/2003	42	25.80	-4.9%	05/14/2004	5
Average:				-16.5%			-5.1%		23		-12.9%		42
Median:				-14.9%			-4.9%		25		-8.3%		35

CHART 69–Preferred Stock Regression Analysis, Alcoa pf A
1998-2005

CHART 70–Preferred Stock Regression Analysis, Consolidated Edison pf A
1998-2005

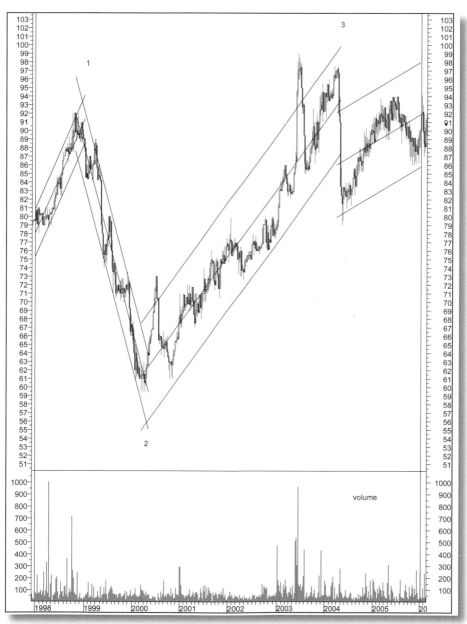

CHART 71–Preferred Stock Regression Analysis, Merrill Lynch pf B
1998-2005

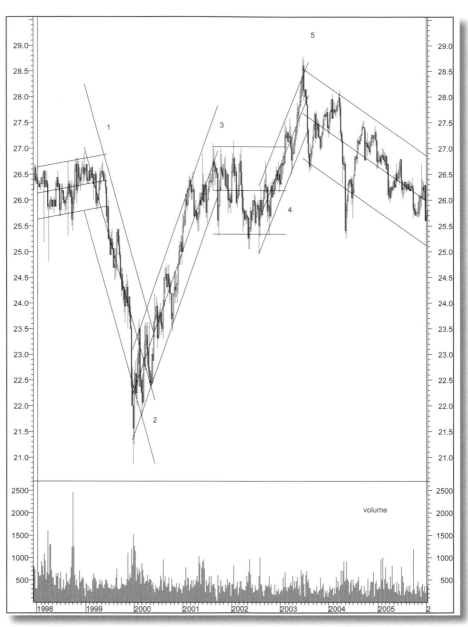

Created in MetaStock from Equis International

MOVING AVERAGES

In analyzing the simple, weighted and exponential moving averages for 10, 20, and 40 weeks, the first objective was to identify the moving averages that had the fewest false signals without the need for filters that could delay the effectiveness of a signal for long-term trend changes. As can be seen on CHARTS 72-77, the 10- and 20-week moving averages would require a filter, such as the 2-week or 3% penetration rule, to be a useful long-term indicator. In the 40-week moving averages shown on CHARTS 78-80, of the 26 false signals that were triggered by only one or two moving average types, just one of the signals was from the simple moving average; this helped turn the 40-week simple moving average into the focus of the study.

Signal Rules

- A crossing of both the opening and closing price (candlestick body) above or below the simple moving average.
- Both oversold and overbought signals were used.

CHART 72–Preferred Stock Moving Average Analysis
Alcoa pf A (10-Week)
1998-2005

Alcoa Preferred Price Chart
10-Week Moving Average

weighted ma = red large dots
exponential ma = red small dots
simple ma = red solid line

Created in MetaStock from Equis International

CHART 73–Preferred Stock Moving Average Analysis
Consolidated Edison pf A (10-Week)
1998-2005

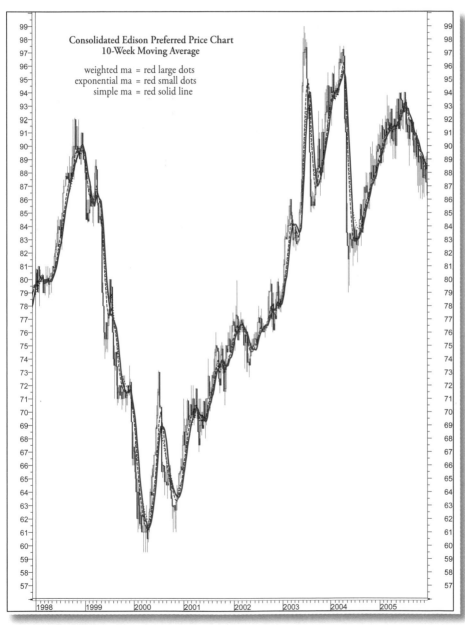

Consolidated Edison Preferred Price Chart
10-Week Moving Average

weighted ma = red large dots
exponential ma = red small dots
simple ma = red solid line

Created in MetaStock from Equis International

CHART 74–Preferred Stock Moving Average Analysis
Merrill Lynch pf B (10-Week)
1998-2005

Merrill Lynch Preferred Price Chart
10-Week Moving Average

weighted ma = red large dots
exponential ma = red small dots
simple ma = red solid line

Created in MetaStock from Equis International

CHART 75–Preferred Stock Moving Average Analysis
Alcoa pf A (20-Week)
1998-2005

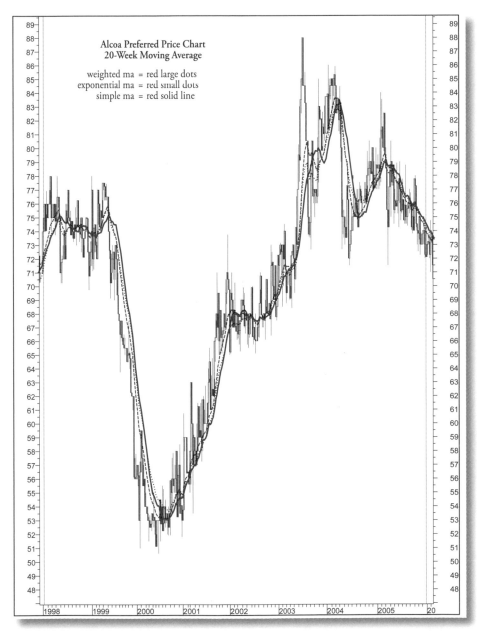

Alcoa Preferred Price Chart
20-Week Moving Average

weighted ma = red large dots
exponential ma = red small dots
simple ma = red solid line

CHART 76–Preferred Stock Moving Average Analysis
Consolidated Edison pf A (20-Week)
1998-2005

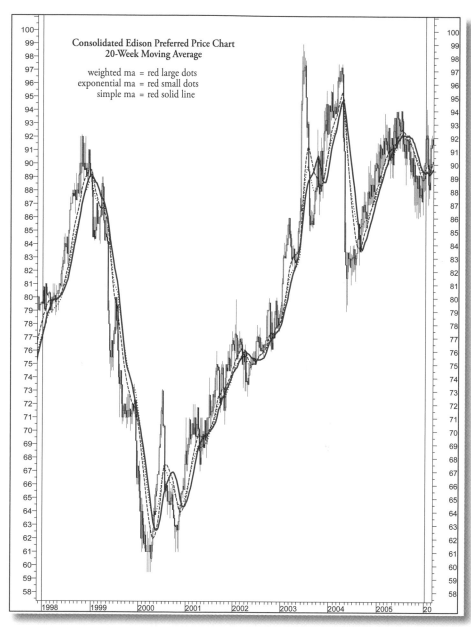

Consolidated Edison Preferred Price Chart
20-Week Moving Average

weighted ma = red large dots
exponential ma = red small dots
simple ma = red solid line

Created in MetaStock from Equis International

CHART 77–Preferred Stock Moving Average Analysis
Merrill Lynch pf B (20-Week)
1998-2005

Merrill Lynch Preferred Price Chart
20-Week Moving Average

weighted ma = red large dots
exponential ma = red small dots
simple ma = red solid line

Created in MetaStock from Equis International

CHART 78–Preferred Stock Moving Average Analysis
Alcoa pf A (40-Week, Incorrect Crossings)
1998-2005

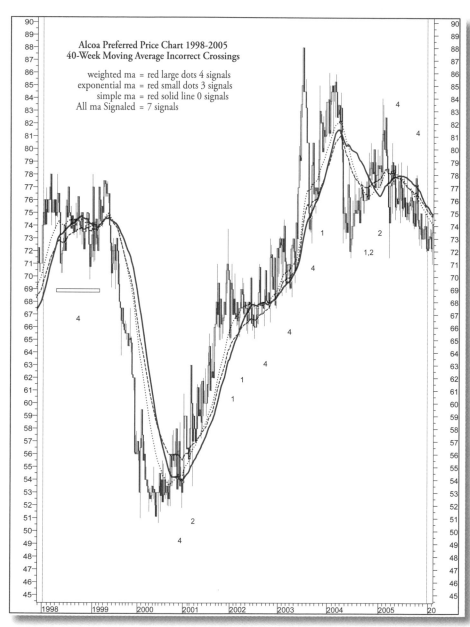

Alcoa Preferred Price Chart 1998-2005
40-Week Moving Average Incorrect Crossings

weighted ma = red large dots 4 signals
exponential ma = red small dots 3 signals
simple ma = red solid line 0 signals
All ma Signaled = 7 signals

CHART 79–Preferred Stock Moving Average Analysis
Consolidated Edison pf A (40-Week, Incorrect Crossings)
1998-2005

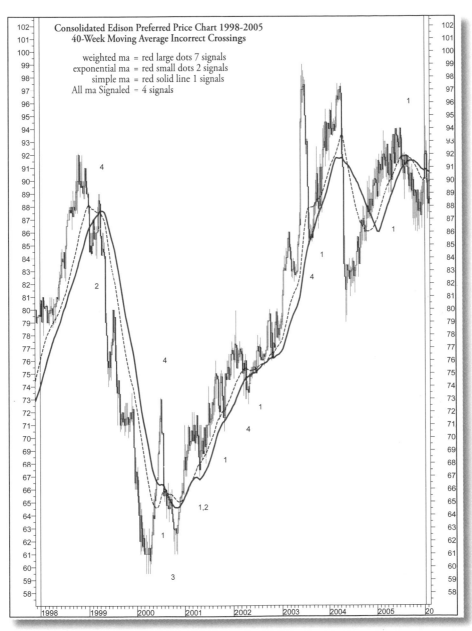

Consolidated Edison Preferred Price Chart 1998-2005
40-Week Moving Average Incorrect Crossings

weighted ma = red large dots 7 signals
exponential ma = red small dots 2 signals
simple ma = red solid line 1 signals
All ma Signaled – 4 signals

Created in MetaStock from Equis International

CHART 80–Preferred Stock Moving Average Analysis
Merrill Lynch pf B (40-Week, Incorrect Crossings)
1998-2005

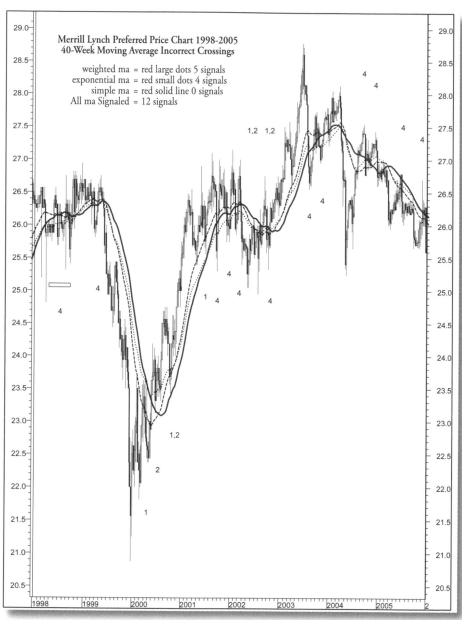

Merrill Lynch Preferred Price Chart 1998-2005
40-Week Moving Average Incorrect Crossings

weighted ma = red large dots 5 signals
exponential ma = red small dots 4 signals
simple ma = red solid line 0 signals
All ma Signaled = 12 signals

Research Summary (TABLE 15, CHARTS 81-83)

The results varied significantly for the three stocks. In the case of Merrill Lynch and Alcoa, a very small number of signals preceded a major change in trend (20% and 24%). In other words, the moving averages unfiltered on these two stocks presented too many false signals to be of any use in identifying major long-term trend changes. In the case of Consolidated Edison, there were six oversold and six overbought completed signals of which 31% of the signals were accurate in indicating the future trend. Both sets of signals proved ineffective to use in a systematic fashion without confirmation from other moving average research (i.e., WIPSI™ studies).

TABLE 15–Preferred Stock 40-Week Simple Moving Average Analysis
Consolidated Edison pf A
1998-2005

Preferred Stock 40 Week Moving Average - Consolidated Edison pr A:

Signal:	Price:	Signal Date:	Total Move's High:	%	High Date:	From Previous Low:	%	Date:	Duration Weeks:	To OB Signal:	%	Date:	Duration Weeks:
Oversold													
2	88.25	04/01/1999								84.25	-4.5%	04/16/1999	2
4	68.75	06/16/2000	99.00	44.0%	06/13/2003	59.50	15.5%	04/14/2000	9	66.00	-4.0%	08/04/2000	7
6	65.25	09/22/2000								63.50	-2.7%	10/06/2000	2
8	65.5	12/08/2000								73.75	12.6%	04/19/2002	71
10	75.5	05/31/2002								83.50	10.6%	04/30/2004	100
12	88.5	11/12/2004	93.95	6.2%	06/02/2005	79.00	12.0%	06/13/2003	74	90.40	2.1%	09/09/2005	43
Average:				25.1%			13.8%		42		2.4%		38
Median:				25.1%			13.8%		42		-0.3%		25

			Low:			High:				To OS Signal			
Overbought:													
1	85	01/22/1999								88.25	3.8%	04/01/1999	10
3	84.25	04/16/1999	59.50	-29.4%	04/14/2000	92.13	-8.6%	10/23/1998	25	68.75	-18.4%	06/16/2000	61
5	66	08/04/2000								65.25	-1.1%	09/22/2000	7
7	63.5	10/06/2000								65.50	3.1%	12/08/2000	9
9	73.75	04/19/2002								75.50	2.4%	05/31/2002	6
11	83.5	04/30/2004	79.00	-5.4%	05/14/2004	99.00	-15.7%	06/13/2003	46	88.50	6.0%	11/12/2004	28
13	PENDING												
Average:				-17.4%			-12.1%		36		-0.7%		20
Median:				-17.4%			-12.1%		36		2.8%		9

CHART 81–Preferred Stock Moving Average Analysis
Alcoa pf A (40-Week)
1998-2005

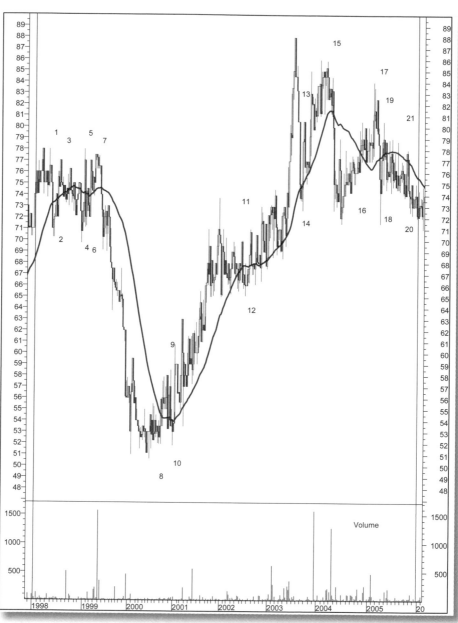

Created in MetaStock from Equis International

CHART 82–Preferred Stock Moving Average Analysis
Consolidated Edison pf A (40-Week)
1998-2005

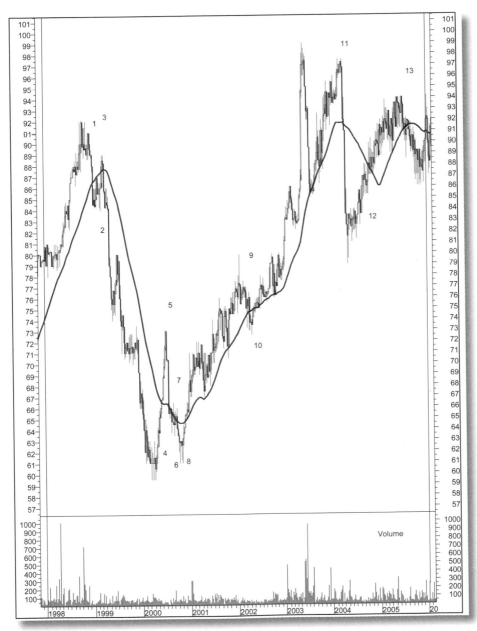

Created in MetaStock from Equis International

CHART 83–Preferred Stock Moving Average Analysis
Merrill Lynch pf B (40-Week)
1998-2005

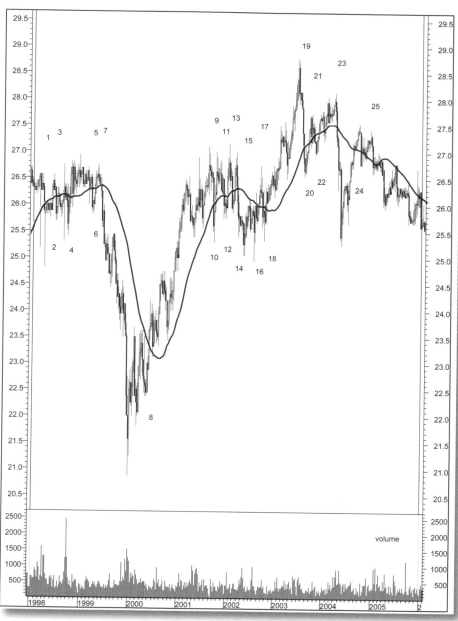

OSCILLATORS

The Wilder Relative Strength (RSI) and Stochastic Indicators were picked because of their popularity with investors. Although these oscillators are usually used in "sideways" markets (i.e., trading ranges), the focus was on whether these indicators would prove useful for providing effective long-term signals in all market conditions.

RSI Signal Rules

- The 14 periods calculation was used.
- The focus was placed on 70 and 30 crossover points.
- The first signal was used with secondary signals used only for confirmation.
- Both overbought and oversold signals were observed.

Research Summary (Table 16, Charts 84-86)

There were five oversold and five overbought completed signals. Although both sets of signals preceded significant moves (oversold 31.4%, overbought -16.4%), when the two signals were used together they were ineffective in providing a completion signal. In other words, this indicator can't be used by itself to provide consistent signals of changes in long-term trends.

Table 16–Preferred Stock RSI (Wilder) Analysis
1998-2005

Preferred Stocks RSI Accurate Signals:

Signal:	Price:	Signal Date:	Total Move's High:	%	High Date:	Duration Weeks:	From Previous Low:	%	Date	Duration Weeks:
Oversold (OS):										
AA1	56.5	01/28/2000	88.00	55.8%	07/02/2003	179	51.00	10.8%	01/28/2000	0
ED5	61.5	04/20/2000	99.00	61.0%	06/13/2003	164	59.50	3.4%	03/17/2000	5
ED11	83.42	05/21/2004	93.95	12.6%	06/02/2005	54	79.00	5.6%	05/14/2004	1
MER4	22.5	01/07/2000	27.15	20.7%	01/18/2002	106	20.88	7.8%	12/31/1999	1
MER7	25.8	05/14/2004	27.54	6.7%	09/24/2004	19	25.25	2.2%	05/14/2004	0
Average:				31.4%		104		5.9%		1
Median:				20.7%		106		5.6%		1
			Low:				High:			
Overbought (OB):										
AA3	88	07/02/2003	71.50	-18.8%	03/24/2005	90	88.00	0.0%	07/02/2003	0
ED2	89.75	10/30/1998	59.50	-33.7%	03/17/2000	72	92.13	-2.6%	10/23/1998	1
ED10	92.75	07/11/2003	79.00	-14.8%	05/14/2004	44	99.00	-6.3%	06/13/2003	4
MER5	26.15	03/09/2001	24.95	-4.6%	07/26/2002	72	27.15	-3.7%	01/18/2002	-45
MER6	28.13	06/27/2003	25.25	-10.2%	05/14/2004	46	28.78	-2.3%	06/20/2003	1
Average:				-16.4%		65		-3.0%		-8
Median:				-14.8%				-2.6%		1

CHART 84–Preferred Stock RSI Analysis
Alcoa pf A
1998-2005

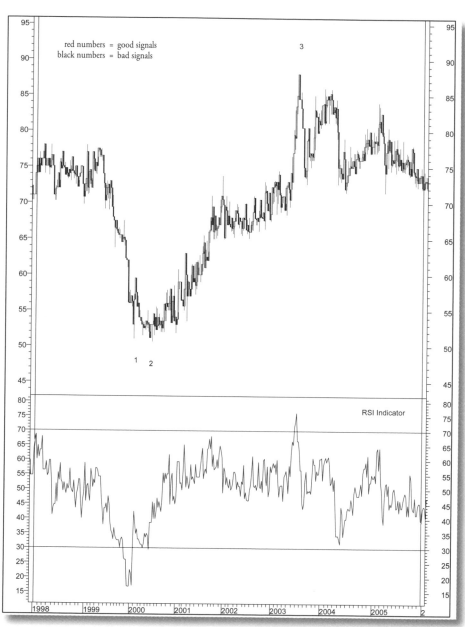

red numbers = good signals
black numbers = bad signals

RSI Indicator

CHART 85–Preferred Stock RSI Analysis
Consolidated Edison pf A
1998-2005

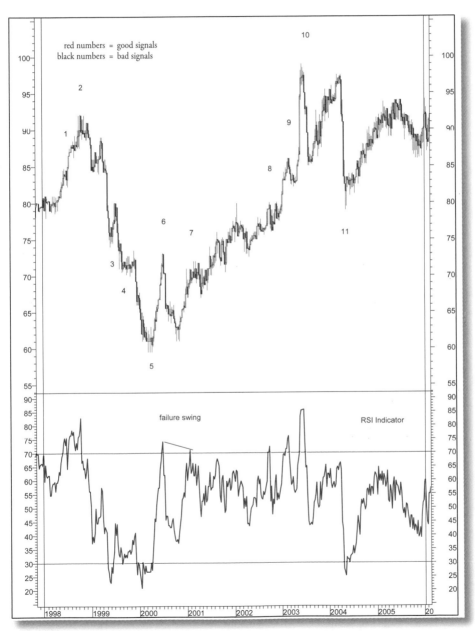

Created in MetaStock from Equis International

CHART 86–Preferred Stock RSI Analysis
Merrill Lynch pf B
1998-2005

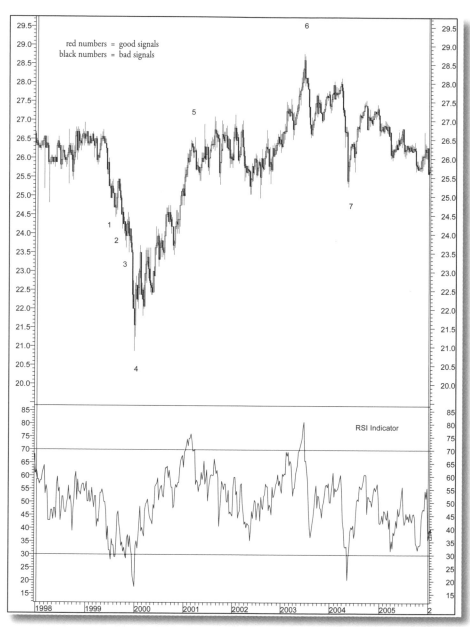

red numbers = good signals
black numbers = bad signals

RSI Indicator

Slow Stochastic Signal Rules

- A 14 period k% calculation with the 3 period average of d% was used.
- The focus was placed 80 and 20 values with a crossing of the %k line below and above %d line.
- Both overbought and oversold signals were observed.

Research Summary (CHARTS 87-89)

The Stochastic Indicator was much more sensitive than the RSI indicator with approximately 74 individual signals among the three stocks. With such a large number of signals and no filtering, the number of false signals made this an unreliable long-term indicator.

CHART 87–Preferred Stock Stochastic Analysis
Alcoa pf A
1998-2005

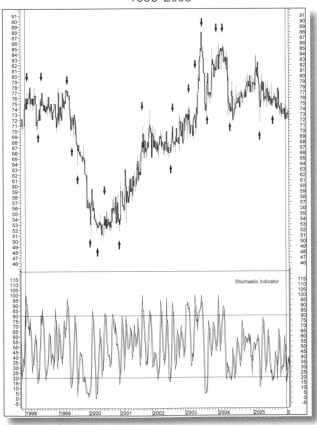

Created in MetaStock from Equis International

CHART 88–Preferred Stock Stochastic Analysis
Consolidated Edison pf A
1998-2005

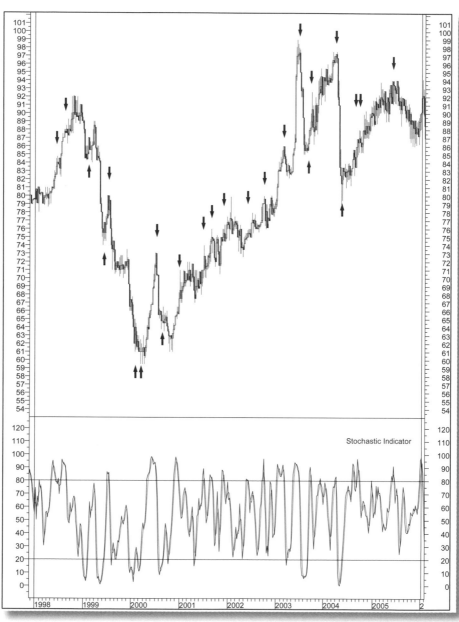

Created in MetaStock from Equis International

CHART 89–Preferred Stock Stochastic Analysis
Merrill Lynch pf B
1998-2005

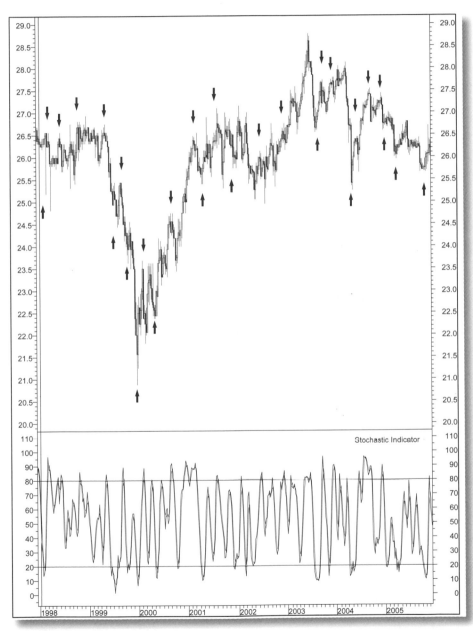

Created in MetaStock from Equis International

RELATIVE STRENGTH (RATIO CHARTS)

To make direct price movement comparisons of the preferred stocks with the issuer's common stocks, the WIPSI, and other preferred stocks, ratio charts were developed.

Preferred Stocks/Common Stock Ratio (CHARTS 90-92)

Although the charts are vastly different, the trendlines here indicate that two of the preferreds gained momentum during the 2000-2002 bear market versus the common stocks.

CHART 90–Alcoa pf A/Alcoa Common Stock Ratio
1998-2005

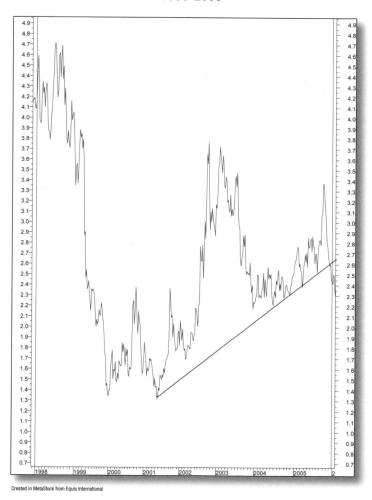

Created in MetaStock from Equis International

CHART 91–Consolidated Edison pf A/Consolidated Edison Common Stock Ratio
1998-2005

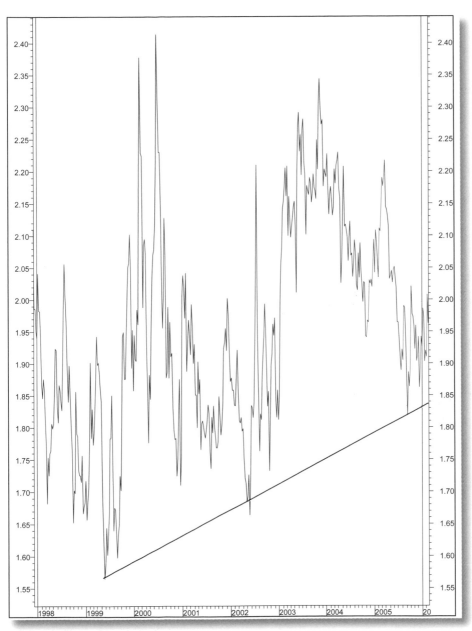

Created in MetaStock from Equis International

CHART 92–Merrill Lynch pf B/Merrill Lynch Common Stock Ratio
1998-2005

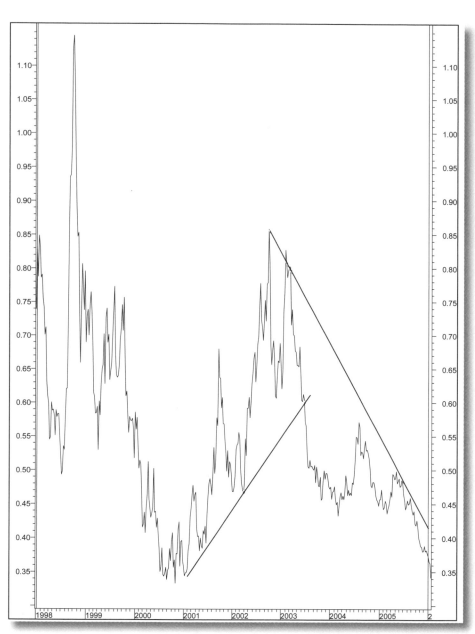

Created in MetaStock from Equis International

Preferred Stocks/WIPSI™ Ratio (CHARTS 93-95)

The ratio charts clearly show weakness in the three preferred stocks versus the WIPSI since 1998.

CHART 93–Alcoa pf A/WIPSI Ratio
1998-2005

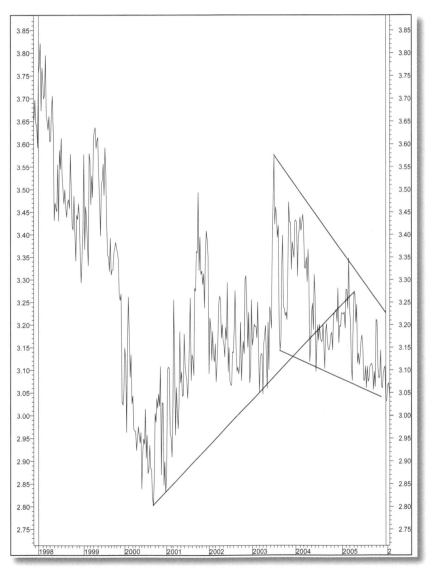

CHART 94–Consolidated Edison pf A/WIPSI™ Ratio
1998-2005

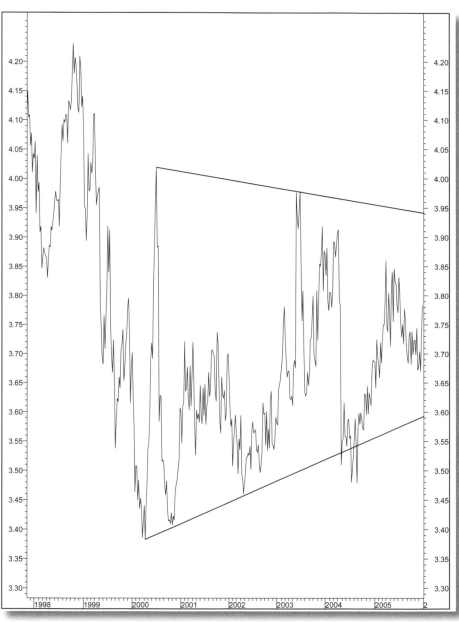

Created in MetaStock from Equis International

CHART 95—Merrill Lynch pf B/WIPSI Ratio
1998-2005

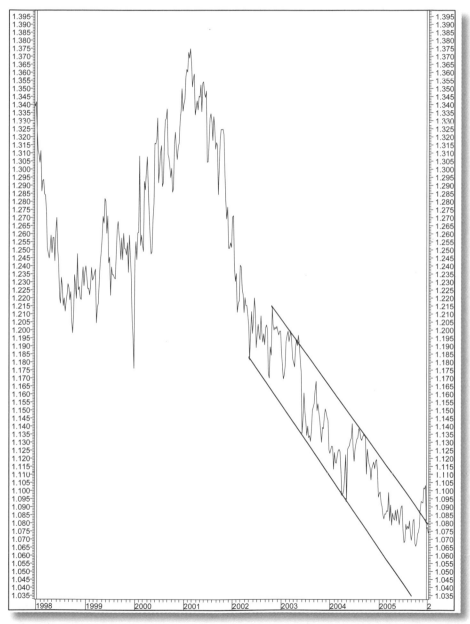

Created in MetaStock from Equis International

Preferred Stocks/Other Preferred Stocks (CHARTS 96-97)

Extreme changes in the price relationships can be clearly seen on the charts. For instance, Merrill Lynch Preferred Series B was at a significant discount to the Preferred Series C in late 1999. Another example: the very high premium that the Alcoa Preferred Series A was at in mid-2004 versus the DuPont Preferred Series B stock.

CHART 96–Merrill Lynch pf B/Merrill Lynch pf C Ratio
1998-2005

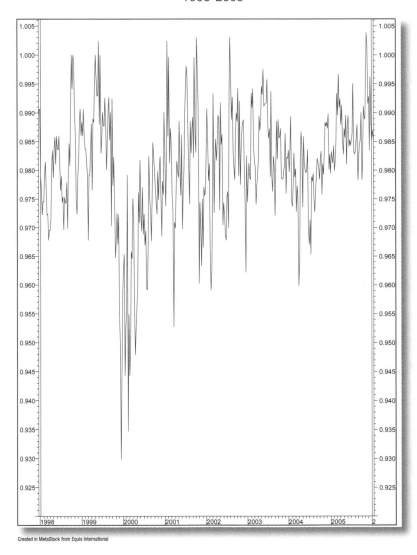

Created in MetaStock from Equis International

CHART 97–Alcoa pf A/Dupont pf B Ratio
1998-2005

FUNDAMENTAL AND RATINGS ANALYSIS

Like bond analysis, reviewing an issuer's fundamentals and ratings is useful in the selection process of new preferreds. It can also help confirm signals in some of the indicators mentioned above. TABLE 17 is a fundamental analysis checklist to evaluate the financial strength of the companies using Valueline's research. The preferred stocks used in this study are old, well-known companies that are industry leaders. They have a long history of profitability, honoring dividend obligations, and a balanced capital structure. However, if they develop a significant number of negative factors in the future, they will usually be removed from the portfolio.

All issues have high S&P ratings, which implies that they have a high probability of honoring their financial commitments to the stockholders now and in the future (TABLE 18).

Fundamental and rating analysis should be reviewed at least annually, or if there is unusual price volatility of the investments as a means to confirm any decision to sell an existing investment.

Table 17—Fundamental Analysis Checklist

Corporate Bond and Preferred Stock Negative Factors

MAJOR

Private Company	(no financial information)
Common Stock Price	Within 10% of 52-week low
Common Stock Price	Below $3.00 per share
Earnings	Three years of losses out of of last five years
Cashflow	Three years of losses out of of last five years
Earnings	Big losses in last two years
Cashflow	Big losses in last two years
Earnings	Losses expected this year
Cashflow	Losses expected this year
Debt to Capital Ratio	More than 75%
Shares Outstanding	High levels of dilution
Valueline Safety Rating	4 or 5
Valueline Financial Strength	Less than B
Negative Accounting Notes and Other Concerns	

MINOR

Revenue	Reduction expected this year
Earnings	Reduction expected this year
Cashflow	Reduction expected this year
Common Dividends	Reduction expected this year
Operating Margin	Less than 7%
Long-term Debt vs Equity	10% increase in debt and reduction in equity
Common Dividend Payout Ratio	Greater than 100%
Revenue	Less than $500 million
Valueline Earnings Predictability	Less than 60
S&P Rating	Lowered

TABLE 18–S&P Corporate Rating Interpretations

Common Stock	Preferreds/ Bonds	General Interpretation
A+	AAA+	Risk Free
	AAA	
	AAA-	
A	AA+	
	AA	
	AA-	
	A+	
	A	
A-	A-	Investment Grade ↑
B+	BBB+	
	BBB	
	BBB-	
B	BB+	
	BB	Medium Grade
	BB-	
B-	B+	
	B	
	NR	"Junk" Rated ↓
	B-	
C+	CCC+	
	CCC	
	CCC-	
C	CC+	
	CC	
	CC-	
C-	C+	
	C	
	C-	
D	D	Default

☐ Preferreds used in study

RESEARCH CONCLUSIONS

Technical analysis can be effectively and efficiently used on preferred stocks and the Winans International Preferred Stock Index™ (WIPSI™) to identify long-term trends, changes in long-term trends, and overbought/oversold situations. And the technical approaches studied had very different outcomes on both the WIPSI and the preferred stocks selected for this analysis:

Trendline Analysis (Tables 19-20)

Long-term trendlines were easy to identify and worked well on both the WIPSI™ and the preferred stocks selected. It showed that by using trendlines, overbought and oversold conditions could be identified in a timely manner from the high or low of the move.

Table 19–WIPSI Trendline Analysis
1981-2005

Signal:	Price:	Signal Date:	Total Move's High:	%	High Date:	Duration Weeks:	From Previous Low:	%	Date	Duration Weeks:	To OB Signal:	%	Date	Duration Weeks:
Oversold (OS):														
0	7.89	02/19/1981	10.60	34.3%	05/06/1983	115	7.88	0.1%	09/25/1981	-31	10.43	32.2%	06/10/1983	120
2	9.04	07/27/1984	15.29	69.1%	02/06/1987	132	9.00	0.4%	07/27/1984	0	14.70	62.6%	04/10/1987	141
5	12.91	05/26/1989	14.17	9.8%	11/24/1989	26	12.66	2.0%	05/19/1989	1	13.87	7.4%	01/26/1990	35
7	13.69	12/21/1990	18.50	35.1%	10/22/1993	148	13.28	3.1%	10/19/1990	9	17.31	26.4%	03/25/1994	170
9	15.36	01/27/1995	17.98	17.1%	02/09/1996	54	14.79	3.9%	12/30/1994	4	17.36	13.0%	03/01/1996	57
10	16.95	07/26/1996	21.80	28.6%	12/01/1998	123	16.49	2.8%	09/13/1996	-7	21.34	25.9%	04/23/1999	143
12	18.09	05/05/2000	24.97	38.0%	03/26/2004	203	17.64	2.6%	03/17/2000	7	24.72	36.7%	04/09/2004	205
Average:				33.2%		114		2.1%		-2		29.2%		124
			Total Move's Low:		Low Date:		From Previous High:				To OS Signal:			
Overbought (OB):														
1	10.43	06/10/1983	9.00	-13.7%	07/27/1984	59	10.60	-1.6%	05/06/1983	5	9.04	-13.3%	07/27/1984	59
3	10.97	06/28/1985	10.74	-2.1%	10/04/1985	14	11.25	-2.5%	06/21/1985	1				
4	14.7	04/10/1987	12.83	-12.7%	10/30/1987	29	15.29	-3.9%	02/06/1987	9	12.91	-12.2%	05/26/1989	111
6	13.87	01/26/1990	13.26	-4.4%	05/18/1990	16	14.18	-2.2%	11/24/1989	9	13.69	-1.3%	12/21/1990	47
8	17.31	03/25/1994	14.79	-14.6%	12/30/1994	40	18.50	-6.4%	10/22/1993	22	15.36	-11.3%	01/27/1995	44
9.5	17.36	03/01/1996	16.49	-5.0%	09/13/1996	28	17.98	-3.4%	02/09/1996	3	16.95	-2.4%	07/26/1996	
11	21.34	04/23/1999	17.64	-17.3%	03/17/2000	47	21.80	-2.1%	02/01/1998	64	18.09	-15.2%	05/05/2000	54
13	not confirmed by yield chart													
14	24.72	04/09/2004	22.86	-7.5%	05/24/2004	6	24.97	-1.0%	03/26/2004	2				
15	pending													
Average:				-10.0%		33		-3.2%		16		-9.3%		63

Table 20–Preferred Stock Trendline Analysis
1998-2005

Signal:	Price:	Signal Date:	Total Move's High:	%	High Date:	From Previous Low:	%	Date	Duration Weeks:	To OB Signal:	%	Date	Duration Weeks:
Oversold (OS):													
AA2	54.5	07/18/2000	88.00	61.5%	07/02/2003	50.63	7.6%	07/11/2000	1	88.00	61.5%	07/02/2003	154
AA4	78.5	09/12/2003	85.90	9.4%	03/04/2004	72.75	7.9%	09/12/2003	0	75.00	-4.5%	04/30/2004	33
AA6	73	06/18/2004	84.00	15.1%	02/04/2005	71.50	2.1%	06/18/2004	0	79.50	8.9%	03/02/2005	37
AA8	Pending												
ED2	63.75	05/12/2000	99.00	55.3%	06/13/2003	59.50	7.1%	03/30/2000	6	95.01	49.0%	07/03/2003	164
ED3	72.55	08/10/2001	99.00	36.5%	06/13/2003	59.50	21.9%	03/30/2000	71	95.01	31.0%	07/03/2003	99
ED6	92.35	11/21/2003	97.05	5.1%	04/08/2004	85.03	8.6%	08/08/2003	15	91.00	-1.5%	04/23/2004	22
ED8	83.42	05/21/2004	93.25	11.8%	07/15/2005	79.00	5.6%	05/14/2004	1	93.25	11.8%	07/15/2005	60
MER2	22.88	05/26/2000	28.78	25.8%	06/20/2004	20.88	9.6%	12/31/1999	21	27.25	19.1%	04/25/2003	152
MER3	Not Confirmed by Volume												
MER3.5	27.25	04/25/2003	28.78	5.6%	06/20/2003	26.50	2.8%	04/25/2003	0	27.14	-0.4%	04/08/2004	50
MER5	25.8	05/14/2004	27.54	6.7%	09/24/2004	25.50	1.2%	05/14/2004	0	27.15	5.2%	12/23/2004	32
Average:				23.3%			7.5%		12		18.0%		80
Median:				13.4%			7.4%		1		10.3%		55
			Low:			High:				To OS Signal			
Overbought (OB):													
AA1	68	07/29/1999	50.63	-25.5%	07/11/2000	78.00	-12.8%	01/08/1999	29	54.50	-19.9%	07/18/2000	51
AA3	88	07/02/2003	75.00	-14.8%	04/30/2004	88.00	0.0%	07/02/2003	0	78.50	-10.8%	09/12/2003	10
AA5	75	04/30/2004	74.25	-1.0%	03/24/2005	88.00	-14.8%	07/02/2003	43	73.00	-2.7%	06/18/2004	7
AA7	79.5	03/02/2005	74.25	-6.6%	03/24/2005	84.00	-5.4%	02/04/2005	4	74.25	-6.6%	03/24/2005	3
ED1	84.25	04/16/1999	59.50	-29.4%	03/30/2000	92.00	-8.4%	10/30/1998	24	63.75	-24.3%	05/12/2000	56
ED4	95.01	07/03/2003	85.03	-10.5%	08/08/2003	99.00	-4.0%	06/13/2003	3	92.35	-2.8%	11/21/2003	20
ED5	85.8	08/08/2003	85.03	-0.9%	08/08/2003	99.00	-13.3%	03/30/2000	175	92.35	7.6%	11/21/2003	15
ED7	91	04/23/2004	79.00	-13.2%	05/14/2004	97.05	-6.2%	04/23/2004	0	83.42	-8.3%	05/21/2004	4
ED9	Pending												
MER1	25.88	06/18/1999	20.88	-19.3%	12/31/1999	26.50	-2.3%	12/24/1998	25	22.88	-11.6%	05/26/2000	49
MER4	27.14	04/08/2004	25.25	-7.0%	05/14/2004	28.78	-5.7%	06/20/2003	42	25.80	-4.9%	05/14/2004	5
MER6	Pending												
Average:				-12.8%			-7.3%		34		-8.4%		22
Median:				-11.8%			-6.0%		25		-7.5%		13

Standard Error Channels (TABLES 21-22)

These channels worked well with both the WIPSI and the stocks for oversold signals. And overbought signals tended to lag when compared to conventional trendlines.

TABLE 21—WIPSI Regression and Standard Error Analysis
1981-2005

WIPSI Regression/Standard Error Analysis:

Signal:	Number:	Price:	Signal Date:	Total Move's High:	%	High Date:	Duration Weeks:	From Previous Low:	%	Date	Duration Weeks:	To OB Signal:	%	Date	Duration Weeks:
Oversold (OS)	1	8.38	05/14/1982	10.60	26.5%	05/06/1983	51	7.90	6.1%	02/12/1982	13	10.17	21.4%	07/29/1983	63
	3	9.64	11/09/1984	15.30	58.7%	02/06/1987	117	9.00	7.1%	07/27/1984	15	13.80	43.2%	05/15/1987	131
	5	13.65	07/07/1989	18.50	35.5%	10/15/1993	223	12.66	7.8%	05/19/1989	7	16.99	24.5%	04/08/1994	248
	7	15.91	04/14/1995	17.98	13.0%	02/09/1996	43	14.79	7.6%	12/30/1994	15	16.95	6.5%	04/19/1996	53
	9	18.09	06/13/1997	21.80	20.5%	12/04/1998	77	16.49	9.7%	09/13/1996	39	21.53	19.0%	12/25/1998	80
	11	18.05	06/30/2000	24.97	38.3%	03/26/2004	195	17.64	2.3%	03/17/2000	15	23.79	31.8%	04/30/2004	200
Average:					32.1%		118		6.8%		17		24.4%		129
Median:					31.0%		97		7.3%		15		22.9%		106

Overbought (OB):				Total Move's Low:						High:		To OS Signal:			
	2	10.17	07/29/1983	9.00	-11.5%	07/27/1984	52	10.60	-4.1%	05/06/1983	12	9.64	-5.2%	11/09/1984	67
	4	13.8	05/15/1987	12.66	-8.3%	05/19/1989	105	15.30	-9.8%	02/06/1987	14	13.65	-1.1%	07/07/1989	112
	6	16.99	04/08/1994	14.79	-12.9%	12/30/1994	38	18.50	-8.2%	10/15/1993	25	15.91	-6.4%	04/14/1995	53
	8	16.95	04/19/1996	16.49	-2.7%	09/13/1996	21	17.98	-5.7%	02/09/1996	10	18.09	6.7%	06/13/1997	60
	10	21.53	12/25/1998	17.64	-18.1%	03/17/2000	64	21.80	-1.2%	12/04/1998	3	18.05	-16.2%	06/30/2000	79
	12	23.79	04/30/2004												
Average					-10.7%		56		-5.8%		13		-4.4%		74
Median					-11.5%		52		-5.7%		12		-5.2%		67

TABLE 22—Preferred Stock Regression and Standard Error Analysis
1998-2005

Preferred Stocks Regression/Standard Error Analysis:

Signal:	Price:	Signal Date:	Total Move's High:	%	High Date:	From Previous Low:	%	Date	Duration Weeks:	To OB Signal:	%	Date	Duration Weeks:
Oversold													
AA1	54.5	07/18/2000	88.00	61.5%	07/02/2003	50.63	7.6%	07/11/2000	1	88.00	61.5%	07/02/2003	154
ED5	63.75	05/12/2000	99.00	55.3%	06/13/2003	59.50	7.1%	03/30/2000	6	95.01	49.0%	07/03/2003	164
ED11	72.55	08/10/2001	99.00	36.5%	06/13/2003	59.50	21.9%	03/30/2000	71	95.01	31.0%	07/03/2003	99
MER4	22.88	05/26/2000	28.78	25.8%	06/20/2003	20.88	9.6%	12/31/1999	21	27.25	19.1%	04/25/2003	152
MER7	27.25	04/25/2003	28.78	5.6%	06/20/2003	26.50	2.8%	04/25/2003	0	27.14	-0.4%	04/08/2004	50
Average:				36.9%			9.8%		20		32.0%		124
Median:				36.5%			7.6%		6		31.0%		152

Overbought:			Low:					High:		To OS Signal			
AA3	Pending												
ED2	84.25	04/16/1999	59.50	-29.4%	03/30/2000	92.00	-8.4%	10/30/1998	24	63.75	-24.3%	05/12/2000	56
ED10	95.01	07/03/2003	85.03	-10.5%	08/08/2003	99.00	-4.0%	06/13/2003	3	92.35	-2.8%	11/21/2003	20
MER5	25.88	06/18/1999	20.88	-19.3%	12/31/1999	26.50	-2.3%	12/24/1998	25	22.88	-11.6%	05/26/2000	49
MER6	27.14	04/08/2004	25.25	-7.0%	05/14/2004	28.78	-5.7%	06/20/2003	42	25.80	-4.9%	05/14/2004	5
Average:				-16.5%			-5.1%		23		-12.9%		42
Median:				-14.9%			-4.9%		25		-8.3%		35

Moving Averages (TABLES 23-24)

The 40-week simple moving average was the most effective moving average of the nine studied. It was significantly more effective on the WIPSI™ than on the individual stocks. The 40-week average could be used on the WIPSI as an independent indicator, and, due to severely lagging signals, it worked well on the stocks when confirmed with WIPSI studies.

TABLE 23–WIPSI 40-Week Simple Moving Average Analysis 1981-2005

Signal:	Number:	Price:	Signal Date	Total Move's High:	%	High Date:	Duration Weeks:	From Previous Low:	%	Date	Duration Weeks:	To OB Signal:	%	Date	Duration Weeks:
Oversold (OS):	1	8.21	03/19/1982	10.60	29.1%	05/06/1983	59	7.90	3.9%	02/19/1982	4	10.01	21.9%	08/05/1983	72
	3	9.64	11/09/1984	15.30	58.7%	02/06/1987	117	9.00	7.1%	07/27/1984	15	14.23	47.6%	04/24/1987	128
	5	13.08	06/02/1989	14.18	8.4%	11/24/1989	25	12.66	3.3%	05/19/1989	2	13.75	5.1%	03/02/1990	39
	7	13.55	11/23/1990	18.49	36.5%	10/23/1993	152	13.27	2.1%	10/19/1990	5	17.75	31.0%	12/31/1993	162
	9	15.89	03/10/1995	17.86	12.4%	02/09/1996	48	14.76	7.7%	12/30/1994	10	17.02	7.1%	04/12/1996	57
	11	17.23	11/08/1996	21.80	26.5%	12/04/1998	108	16.48	4.6%	09/13/1996	8	21.35	23.9%	03/05/1999	121
	13	18.19	08/04/2000	24.97	37.3%	03/26/2004	190	17.75	2.5%	03/17/2000	20	24.05	32.2%	04/23/2004	194
	15	24.11	10/01/2004	24.87	3.2%	02/11/2005	19	22.93	5.1%	05/14/2004	20	24.14	0.1%	03/25/2005	25
Average:					26.5%		90		4.5%		11		21.1%		100
Median:					27.8%		84		4.2%		9		22.9%		97
				Low:				High:				To OS Signal			
Overbought (OB):	2	10.01	08/05/1983	9.00	-10.1%	07/27/1984	51	10.60	-5.6%	05/06/1983	13	9.64	-3.7%	11/09/1984	66
	4	14.23	04/24/1987	12.66	-11.0%	05/19/1989	108	15.30	-7.0%	02/06/1987	11	13.08	-8.1%	06/02/1989	110
	6	13.75	03/02/1990	13.27	-3.5%	10/19/1990	33	14.18	-3.0%	11/24/1989	14	13.55	-1.5%	11/23/1990	38
	8	17.75	12/31/1993	14.76	-16.8%	12/30/1994	52	18.49	-4.0%	10/23/1993	10	15.89	-10.5%	03/10/1995	62
	10	17.02	04/12/1996	16.48	-3.2%	09/13/1996	22	17.86	-4.7%	02/09/1996	9	17.23	1.2%	11/08/1996	30
	12	21.35	03/05/1999	17.75	-16.9%	03/17/2000	54	21.80	-2.1%	12/04/1998	13	18.19	-14.8%	08/04/2000	74
	14	24.05	04/23/2004	22.93	-4.7%	05/14/2004	3	24.97	-3.7%	03/26/2004	4	24.11	0.2%	10/01/2004	23
Average:					-9.5%		46		-4.3%		11		-5.3%		58
Median:					-10.1%		51		-4.0%		11		-3.7%		62

TABLE 24–Preferred Stock 40-Week Simple Moving Average Analysis Consolidated Edison pf A 1998-2005

Signal:	Price:	Signal Date:	Total Move's High:	%	High Date:	From Previous Low:	%	Date:	Duration Weeks:	To OB Signal:	%	Date:	Duration Weeks:
Oversold													
2	88.25	04/01/1999								84.25	-4.5%	04/16/1999	2
4	68.75	06/16/2000	99.00	44.0%	06/13/2003	59.50	15.5%	04/14/2000	9	66.00	-4.0%	08/04/2000	7
6	65.25	09/22/2000								63.50	-2.7%	10/06/2000	2
8	65.5	12/08/2000								73.75	12.6%	04/19/2002	71
10	75.5	05/31/2002								83.50	10.6%	04/30/2004	100
12	88.5	11/12/2004	93.95	6.2%	06/02/2005	79.00	12.0%	06/13/2003	74	90.40	2.1%	09/09/2005	43
Average:				25.1%			13.8%		42		2.4%		38
Median:				25.1%			13.8%		42		-0.3%		25
			Low:			High:				To OS Signal			
Overbought:													
1	85	01/22/1999								88.25	3.8%	04/01/1999	10
3	84.25	04/16/1999	59.50	-29.4%	04/14/2000	92.13	-8.6%	10/23/1998	25	68.75	-18.4%	06/16/2000	61
5	66	08/04/2000								65.25	-1.1%	09/22/2000	7
7	63.5	10/06/2000								65.50	3.1%	12/08/2000	9
9	73.75	04/19/2002								75.50	2.4%	05/31/2002	6
11	83.5	04/30/2004	79.00	-5.4%	05/14/2004	99.00	-15.7%	06/13/2003	46	88.50	6.0%	11/12/2004	28
13	PENDING												
Average:				-17.4%			-12.1%		36		-0.7%		20
Median:				-17.4%			-12.1%		36		2.8%		9

Oscillators (TABLES 25-26)

Wilder's RSI and Stochastics were studied. Although Stochastic analysis proved the least effective of all the studies performed in this work, RSI was extremely good at identifying oversold conditions on the WIPSI, plus both overbought and oversold conditions in the preferred stocks. This indicator would coordinate well with trendlines, regression, or moving average analysis.

TABLE 25–WIPSI RSI (Wilder) Analysis
1981-2005

Signal:	Number:	price:	Signal date:	Total Move's High:	%	High date:	duration weeks:	From Previous Low:	%	date	duration weeks:
Oversold (OS)	1	8.03	10/31/1981	10.60	32.0%	05/06/1983	79	7.90	1.6%	09/25/1981	5
	2	9.14	07/20/1984	15.30	67.4%	02/06/1987	133	9.04	1.1%	07/20/1984	0
	3	13.19	11/06/1987	14.18	7.5%	11/24/1989	107	12.83	2.8%	10/30/1987	1
	4	13.43	05/25/1990	18.51	37.8%	10/15/1993	177	13.26	1.3%	05/18/1990	1
	5	16.77	05/20/1994	21.80	30.0%	12/04/1990	237	14.78	13.5%	12/30/1994	32
	6	18.01	03/24/2000	24.97	38.6%	03/26/2004	209	17.64	2.1%	03/17/2000	1
	7	23.33	05/28/2004	24.87	6.6%	02/11/2005	37	22.86	2.1%	05/14/2004	2
Average:					31.4%		140		3.5%		-3
Median:					32.0%		133		2.1%		1

TABLE 26–Preferred Stock RSI (Wilder) Analysis
1998-2005

Signal:	Price:	Signal Date:	Total Move's High:	%	High Date:	Duration Weeks:	From Previous Low:	%	Date	Duration Weeks:
Oversold (OS):										
AA1	56.5	01/28/2000	88.00	55.8%	07/02/2003	179	51.00	10.8%	01/28/2000	0
ED5	61.5	04/20/2000	99.00	61.0%	06/13/2003	164	59.50	3.4%	03/17/2000	5
ED11	83.42	05/21/2004	93.95	12.6%	06/02/2005	54	79.00	5.6%	05/14/2004	1
MER4	22.5	01/07/2000	27.15	20.7%	01/18/2002	106	20.88	7.8%	12/31/1999	1
MER7	25.8	05/14/2004	27.54	6.7%	09/24/2004	19	25.25	2.2%	05/14/2004	0
Average:				31.4%		104		5.9%		1
Median:				20.7%		106		5.6%		1
			Low:				High:			
Overbought (OB):										
AA3	88	07/02/2003	71.50	-18.8%	03/24/2005	90	88.00	0.0%	07/02/2003	0
ED2	89.75	10/30/1998	59.50	-33.7%	03/17/2000	72	92.13	-2.6%	10/23/1998	1
ED10	92.75	07/11/2003	79.00	-14.8%	05/14/2004	44	99.00	-6.3%	06/13/2003	4
MER5	26.15	03/09/2001	24.95	-4.6%	07/26/2002	72	27.15	-3.7%	01/18/2002	-45
MER6	28.13	06/27/2003	25.25	-10.2%	05/14/2004	46	28.78	-2.3%	06/20/2003	1
Average:				-16.4%		65		-3.0%		-8
Median:				-14.8%				-2.6%		1

Relative Strength Ratios

All six of the ratio charts studied proved useful in identifying changes in momentum between different investments. They could help an investor select an issuer's strongest-performing preferred, as well as assist in timing investments between preferred stocks and corporate bonds

Fundamental and Ratings Analysis

This analysis proved useful as a preliminary screen for investment candidates, as well as a way to confirm the reasons for unusual price volatility of an existing investment holding.

Although it is still baffling why investment analysts have largely neglected preferred stocks, effective techniques have been discovered that give investors ways to identify general trends in preferred stocks through the WIPSI™, as well as individual preferreds. Such tools facilitate a disciplined and systematic approach to buying preferreds. This book has proven that investment analysis can be effectively and efficiently used to aid investors who are interested in preferred stocks.

Summary

This landmark book, the first written on traditional preferred stocks since 1930s, has established that a huge, long-term shift of money toward income investing is under way. It's happening as members of the Baby Boom generation begin to reach retirement age.

Investors are having problems understanding the risks of these investments, as well as how to properly use the statistics, agency ratings, and market benchmarks that are important to income investing. If investors don't "get up to speed" on the advantages and risks of these investments, it could lead to devastating consequences.

Before focusing on preferred stocks, an effort was made to educate investors about the proper ways to use income investments by reviewing the time-tested, basic rules for successful income investing.

This book is about preferred stocks: their historical performance versus other investment types and the advantages and disadvantages of using them. It has been shown that preferreds have generally outperformed corporate bonds and municipal bonds during the past 105 years. And it has been indicated that including them in portfolios should boost the overall returns of those portfolios.

The Winans International Preferred Stock Index™ (WIPSI™), the first preferred stock index dedicated to tracking the price and yield of traditional preferred stocks, is discussed and examined. Later, the WIPSI is depicted as a powerful tool for tracking the preferred stock market, which is valued at a whopping $200 billion. It can also be used to evaluate the past performance of preferred stock versus other investment mediums.

Many technical indicators were used on the WIPSI and individual preferred stocks. The indicators were very effective identifiers of overall price trends and intermediate overbought and oversold conditions.

Everything is brought together in the "Portfolio Management" section, which shows how you can integrate investing in preferreds with other income investments by first establishing a goal, then executing your strategy, and finally by evaluating, monitoring, and periodically rebalancing your income portfolio.

Finally, the practical investment issues surrounding preferreds are briefly reviewed.

Here's one last thought. When you invest in uncommon arenas, such as preferreds, don't be surprised if it's a little unnerving or even downright scary. Wall Street does not continuously promote all types of investments. But the storehouse of knowledge in this book should be empowering. It can help any investor embrace preferred stocks, just like he or she's done with other investments. By using the techniques discussed here, you'll have a great shot at becoming more successful and wealthier than the rest of the investing "herd."

Appendices

WIPSI™ Specifications

INDEX CONSTRUCTION

During 2004 and early 2005, the Winans International (WI) research staff started from scratch and developed, tested, and refined this index through the following steps.

Data Used

Data were gathered from issues of *Barron's*, *The Wall Street Journal*, and the *Standard & Poor's Stock Guides* since 1986.

From *Barron's*, data were used from the Bonds, Market Laboratory on Bonds, and Preferred Stock sections, dating back to January 1986 (the publication did not start listing preferred stocks until mid-2003). Information was retrieved on preferred stocks from issues of *The Wall Street Journal* published since 2001.

To enlarge the period of time being studied, year-end issues of *Standard & Poor's Stock Guide's* Preferred Stock Summaries back to 1990 were gathered.

Data Categorization

The data mentioned above contain both preferred stocks and hybrid investment products listed by the various sources as preferreds, even though they are hybrids. Because the purpose of the WIPSI is to be an index for traditional preferred stocks, we excluded hybrids, floating rate, and convertible preferreds.

The hybrid investments excluded were:
- PINES—Public Income Notes represent general, unsecured, unsubordinated obligations of a company sold to the public in small share amounts, such as $25. They trade on the stock exchanges, pay fixed specified quarterly interest payments, are redeemable at par plus accrued interest at the option of the company after a specified period (generally five years), and mature in 30 to 50 years.
- QUIBS—Quarterly Interest Bonds are a security that is a Morgan Stanley product for a corporate bond sold in small denominations (usually $25 per bond), paying quarterly interest to emulate a Trust Preferred Security, but without the trust.

- QUICS —Quarterly Income Capital Securities are a debt security that is a Lehman Brothers instrument for a corporate debt security sold in small denominations (typically $25 per bond), paying quarterly interest, redeemable at the issuer's option (generally five years and maturing in 30 to 40 years) to emulate a Trust Preferred Security, without the trust.
- QUIDS—Quarterly Income Debt Securities are a debt security that is Goldman Sachs & Company product for a corporate debt security sold in small denominations (almost always $25), paying quarterly interest, redeemable at the issuers option (usually in five years and maturing in 30 to 40 years) to emulate a Trust Preferred Security, minus the trust.
- QUIPS—Quarterly Income Preferred Securities is a Goldman Sachs & Company product for a Trust Preferred Security.
- TRUPS—Trust Preferred Securities is a Salomon Smith Barney/ Citibank instrument for a Trust Preferred Security.
- TOPRS—Trust Originated Preferred Securities is a Merrill Lynch product for a Trust Preferred Security.

Note: Hybrids are relatively new financial vehicles (most were created after 1999) that are highly invested in fixed-income securities.

Data Examination
The next task was to identify preferred securities for the WIPSI. WI focused on the companies that normally had preferred shares outstanding during a 14-year span that was studied.

Index Composition
After identifying 57 companies that usually had preferred shares outstanding from 1986-2004, the final selection process for the WIPSI's components was based on the following factors:

Issuer Consistency
The focus was on companies that have historically issued preferred stock. Firms that had preferreds at the beginning and the end of the period examined,

and did not have preferred stock issued for two years within the time were usually excluded.

To make the index useful for long-term analysis, it is important to keep the underlying issuing companies consistently in the index.

Longevity of the Security Itself

Preferred stocks with less than two years of trading history were usually excluded. If an issuing company had more than one preferred stock issued, the one that had been consistently traded for the longest amount of time was chosen.

Call and Convert Features

Preferred stocks, which could be called within one year, or were convertible into common stock, were usually excluded from the WIPSI™. And, there were some preferreds in the index whose call dates were continuous and in perpetuity. Because these securities had been traded for a long time, and there had been no corporate announcements to the contrary, it was believed they wouldn't be called in the foreseeable future.

Trading Activity

Preferreds do not usually trade as often as their counterparts in the world of common stocks. Every proposed component of the WIPSI had to meet a minimum standard of trading activity: It needed to have been traded within the past two weeks in a normal range, compared to the other members of the WIPSI.

Replacement Components

Unlike most market indices, backup preferred stocks were identified as index components. These backups were issued by the same company and had already passed WI's criteria to be a component of the index. To ensure that a called preferred would not have much effect on the index's continuity, each of the replacement securities had price movements that resembled its "matching" original component.

Exclusion from the Index

As a general rule, a security is removed from the index if it does not trade consistently for more than two weeks or is called by the issuer. It is replaced by a backup preferred of the same issuing company, as mentioned in the previous section. The backup securities have different symbols. Data from the removed securities will be kept in the index up to the date of removal, which is when the new security will take over.

Winans International performs an annual review of all preferred stocks in the WIPSI.

Out of the 57 issuers selected from the preliminary analysis, 30 companies passed the selection criteria mentioned above. Their preferred stock was included in the WIPSI. Although it is believed the sample size is sufficient, an annual review of the 27 excluded issuers is conducted to see if they meet the selection criteria. All the price, volume, and yield data for the preferred stocks of the 30 companies were collected (13 companies were trading as far back as 1980): This became the WIPSI starting point.

The number of WIPSI components has gradually increased as follows:

NUMBER	DATE
13	March 1980
14	December 1986
15	January 1994
16	June 1997
17	February 1998
18	September 1998
19	November 1998
20	July 1999
21	June 2001
22, 23, 24	November 2001
25	January 2002
26, 27	June 2002
28	August 2002
29, 30	September 2002

Possible Component Changes

Five issues are callable in 2007. As explained above, backup candidates are available for the called securities. The backups are issued by the same company and have a price movement similar to the original. A called preferred in the index should not have much effect on the continuity of the index.

Index Weighting

The WIPSI™ is an even-weighted index that's based on the average price and yield of its components. This was done for the following reasons:

- Due to the limited sample size of long-term, actively traded preferred securities, a data weighting could create volatility. The volatility wouldn't reflect the true trading nature of the preferreds. For example, a high weighted component can sway the entire index, implying that the overall market is volatile, when the price movement could be issue specific (especially on issues being called).

- Preferred stock is issued in increments of $25, $50, and $100. The price usually does not split. The divisors used to keep the WIPSI even-weighted are easy to maintain and do not have to change. For instance, all $50 par valued preferred stocks in the index are reset to $25 par by dividing the price by two. The par value for this index is $25.

- The process of weighting data is easier to apply in indices for common stocks, where a company usually has only one common stock issued. In the case of preferred stocks, a company can have multiple preferred issues in different sizes in the market at the same time. This raises the question, "What could be used as an effective weighting method for this index?" Do you use the capitalization for the specific preferred or should you use the capitalization for all preferreds in a company's capital structure (even though they may have been issued at different times and could have different levels of liquidity)? Unfortunately, data on called or retired preferred stocks are not available from major data vendors, so this leaves no reliable way to back-test different weighting hypotheses over a suitable period of time.

Note: Value Line's Convertible Index has set a great standard—it's even-weighted, even though it has 612 components.

Calculations

The index's price and yield are calculated daily at 1:15 p.m. Pacific. For the securities that did not trade, the "Last Trade" price is used in putting together the index. Supplemental information, such as average S&P rating, industry coverage percentage, and company revenues, is calculated annually.

WIPSI Use and Licensing

The Winans International Preferred Stock Index™ is also known as the WIPSI™. Both are trademarked. This book and its methodologies are copyright protected against unauthorized duplication. Unauthorized use is prohibited.

Preferred Stock Information

Here are good sources of information on preferred stocks.

Preferred Stocks Availability

- *The Wall Street Journal*
  Daily activity of preferreds.
- *Barron's Financial Weekly*
  Provides a complete list of actively traded issues.
- www.preferredsonline.com
  Shows what is currently offered daily plus
  additional information about the issues.

Corporate, Issue, and Ratings Information

- www.preferredsonline.com
- www.investinginbonds.com
- *Valueline* (monthly)
- www.standardandpoors.com

Technical Analysis

- www.globalfinancialdata.com
- www.bigcharts.com
- www.stockcharts.com
- Metastock software products

Market Benchmarks Information

- www.globalfinancialdata.com
- www.winansintl.com
- www.PreferredsTheBook.com

List of Charts

List of Exhibits

List of Tables

Sources

Written Reference Sources
"Winans International Preferred Stock Index,"
(Winans, Jadhav, Molakides, Gularte) 9/27/2005 (©) (Report)
"The Other Bubble," Winans 10/30/2005 (Report)
"Technical Analysis of Preferred Stocks," Winans 3/20/2006 (Report)

Data Used from the Following Services
Global Financial Data
Dial Data
Reuters
Morningstar

Disclosure Page

These investments are not suitable for everyone. A professional advisor should be consulted about the merits of the investments listed in this book before investing.

Past performance should not be taken as being representative of future results.

The source of the information supplied and formula calculations used are considered reliable and cannot be guaranteed.

All information provided in this book is for informational purposes only. Anything tax-related should be discussed with your accountant before it is used for tax purposes.

Kenneth G. Winans and/or his associates and/or employees may have an interest in the securities herein described and may make purchases or sales of these securities without advance notice at any time.

The amounts and percentages shown are for illustration purposes only and do not reflect actual securities or performance.

The opinions expressed in this book are solely those of Kenneth G. Winans and not those of Winans International Investment Management and Research.

About the Author

"Ken is by far the best stock market commentator that I've heard!"
KNX RADIO LISTENER, MARCH 2005

For more than 24 years, Kenneth G. Winans has conducted extensive investment analyses and designed innovative investment models and strategies. He is a regular guest on various TV and radio shows and has had much of his investment research published by leading magazines and newspapers worldwide. He can be heard every Wednesday 1-1:30 p.m. on Los Angeles' most popular news radio station, CBS affiliate KNX (1070 AM), in a segment called *Wednesdays with Winans*.

In 1992, Ken decided to leave a promising career with Merrill Lynch to launch Winans International. From a spare room in his home, he started the company with approximately $7 million in client assets. WI has approximately 115 investors throughout the United States—personal portfolios, small-business retirement plans, and nonprofit organization investments. As of March 31, 2006, WI's assets under management were $102 million.

He is a member of the Market Technicians Association and completed the Chartered Market Technician (CMT) accreditation program. Ken is also a member of the Chartered Financial Analyst (CFA) Institute. He served as adjunct faculty member of the Graduate School of Business at St. Mary's College of California from 1996-2001. He has a master degree in finance for University of San Francisco, and a bachelor degree in business administration from the University of San Diego.

In 2004, Ken and his wife Debbie founded The W Foundation, a nonprofit organization dedicated to educating the public about the history and future benefits of space exploration. In his spare time, Ken ski-races in the U.S. Ski Association's Masters Program, and collects artifacts from the U.S. space program and antique stock certificates.

Ken and Debbie are longtime residents of the San Francisco Bay area.

Preferreds:
It's not if, but when, you will own them!

To Order
800-310-5389

www.PreferredsTheBook.com